Introducing
Old Testament
Theology

navigates the 'Older' Testament's diversity and interconnections. Bellinger's judicious exegetical insights are matched by his keen conceptual thinking—a perfect combination for a theological introduction. Bellinger has turned a 'lost cause' into a just cause."

—**William P. Brown**, Columbia Theological Seminary

"Reading with the grain and using text-centered approaches, Bellinger invites readers to ponder select theological ideas that he draws out from his reading of 'Older Testament' texts. The volume reinforces the point that readers, grounded in their social locations, create meanings for biblical texts and that all theological content needs to be assessed critically and hermeneutically. The volume elicits questions: What constitutes Old Testament theology? Whose theology is being presented? How is such theology to be understood in the context of the twenty-first-century globalized world?"

—**Carol J. Dempsey**, University of Portland

"Finding a shape for Old Testament theology without allowing that theology to shape the Old Testament is the present challenge of the discipline. We need ways of doing Old Testament theology that have a sense of their own shape and can enter a dialogue with other aspects of Old Testament study without trying to encompass all of them, and this is what Bellinger's work offers. His elegant presentation of creation, covenant, and prophecy keeps the movement of the Old Testament's narrative in view while attending to the complexity and diversity of its literary components. His definition of salvation as 'integrity of life' provides an expansive horizon for viewing the ways texts in the Old Testament engage contemporary questions."

—**Mark McEntire**, Belmont University

"This offering on Old Testament theology is a gift of tradition, of scholarly history, and of current creativity. Bellinger mines the historic conversation on what the words 'Old Testament' and 'theology' mean when they are connected by reminding us of the field of study and the way Scripture leads us into a view of God that illuminates faith. His definitions and examples make the book worth the read, even if one believes they already 'know' Old Testament theology. Let this book, then, be a reintroduction from different vantage points. I hope professors will take it up, offer it to their students, and lean into his creative thinking and expansive grace as he leads us through the text with a paradigm for how to engage the First Testament's words about its God. The book is a gift worth exploring."

—**Valerie Bridgeman**, Methodist Theological School in Ohio

"For a generation, Bill Bellinger has been at the forefront of our shared scholarship on the book of Psalms. Now, near the end of his teaching-scholarly career, he has moved out to a most ambitious undertaking in this book. The hard work of Old Testament theology is elementally to find a model or paradigm that can account for most of the textual material. Bellinger proposes a model that is not unlike a three-legged stool, offered in the parts of creation, covenant, and prophetic proclamation. It is of special interest that Bellinger finds his three accents in the book of Psalms, the text he knows best. In articulating this three-pronged model, Bellinger brings the wisdom of his many years of study. It is clear from this work that the enterprise of Old Testament theology is well, healthy, and demanding. Bellinger's discussion is sure to evoke new explorations and focus attention on canonical matters and the mystery of divine-human interaction that is definitional for the scriptural tradition."

—**Walter Brueggemann**, Columbia Theological Seminary (emeritus)

"Bellinger (who knows his way around the Bible) here presents a shape for Old Testament theology that is founded on, if not centered in, the book of Psalms. 'The key,' Bellinger suggests, 'is to stay as close as is humanly possible to the perspective the Hebrew text articulates about God and divine-human engagement.' He then proceeds to do exactly that by working through the main units and books of the Old Testament, assessing the parts in light of the whole and its larger structure. In the end, Bellinger identifies a kind of three-legged stool, with creation theology, covenant theology, and prophetic theology all supporting a seat that is nothing less than salvation itself. I am confident that this book will prove eminently useful in a wide range of courses on the Old Testament and its theology."

—**Brent A. Strawn**, Duke University

"Bellinger offers an innovative approach to an Old Testament theology. First, the three-legged stool analogy of creation, covenant theology, and prophetic tradition provides readers with tangible 'hooks' on which to hang the seemingly myriad theological ideas present in the Older Testament. And second, using the Psalter as a starting point for exploring this 'stool' provides a superb contextual focus for beginning the study. This volume will be a valuable resource for professors, students, and pastors."

—**Nancy L. deClaissé-Walford**, McAfee School of Theology, Mercer University

"Just as writing an Old Testament theology has been deemed a futile exercise, Bellinger offers an engaging and elegant introduction that deftly

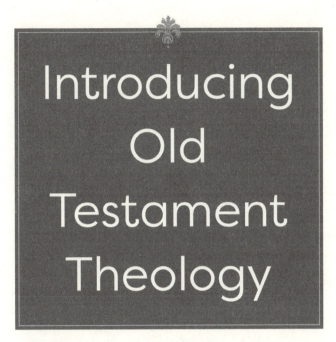

Introducing Old Testament Theology

Creation, Covenant, and Prophecy
in the Divine-Human Relationship

W. H. BELLINGER JR.

B
Baker Academic
a division of Baker Publishing Group
Grand Rapids, Michigan

© 2022 by William H. Bellinger Jr.

Published by Baker Academic
a division of Baker Publishing Group
PO Box 6287, Grand Rapids, MI 49516-6287
www.bakeracademic.com

Printed in the United States of America

Library of Congress Cataloging-in-Publication Data
Names: Bellinger, W. H. (William H.), Jr., 1949– author.
Title: Introducing Old Testament theology : creation, covenant, and prophecy in the divine-human relationship / W. H. Bellinger Jr.
Description: Grand Rapids : Baker Academic, a division of Baker Publishing Group, [2022] | Includes bibliographical references and index.
Identifiers: LCCN 2021046039 | ISBN 9781540961471 (paperback) | ISBN 9781540965523 (casebound) | ISBN 9781493420551 (ebook) | ISBN 9781493420568 (PDF)
Subjects: LCSH: Bible. Old Testament—Theology. | Bible. Old Testament—Criticism, interpretation, etc.
Classification: LCC BS1192.5 .B45 2022 | DDC 230/.0411—dc23
LC record available at https://lccn.loc.gov/2021046039

Baker Publishing Group publications use paper produced from sustainable forestry practices and post-consumer waste whenever possible.

22   23   24   25   26   27   28   7   6   5   4   3   2   1

I dedicate this volume, with gratitude, to my colleagues in the Department of Religion at Baylor University and to Dr. Stephen Breck Reid, professor of Christian Scriptures at George W. Truett Theological Seminary, Baylor University, for his friendship and ongoing dialogue with my scholarly work.

Contents

Preface   xi

Introduction   1

1. Beginnings   19

2. A Shape for Old Testament Theology   45

3. Pentateuch   65

4. Historical Books   99

5. Psalms   117

6. Wisdom   135

7. Prophecy   153

Conclusion   171

Bibliography   181

Subject Index   189

Scripture Index   197

Preface

Readers of this volume are likely those with an interest in the Bible and in particular what the Bible says about God and about faith. The volume will likely find a place in college and seminary classrooms and so as part of the academic study of the Bible. Biblical studies include a variety of perspectives on the Bible, such as historical background or connections and literary questions about the text and how it came to be. Readers may have some background in such academic endeavors with the Bible and now be prepared to take on another area of inquiry—Old Testament theology. The term "theology" literally means a word about God. This area of study typically embraces that in a broad way to talk about faith and the divine-human relationship and implications thereof. In traditional biblical study, attention to the theological dimensions of biblical texts has often been seen as the crowning task of the discipline. This volume will summon the readers' experience with the Old Testament and with theology to explore their relationships. The emphasis will be on the Protestant canon.

Some scholars have abandoned the use of the term "Old Testament" because the adjective is seen to suggest outdated ancient texts with no connections to the twenty-first century. Some fear that the term communicates a supersessionism in which the New Testament completely replaces the Old. The terminological issue has brought several responses.

Some scholars use the term Hebrew Bible or Hebrew Scriptures (though there are some parts in Aramaic) to clarify that these texts originated in Hebrew communities. For those interested in theological concerns in the text, it is problematic that those terms are academic inventions and not tied to any community of faith. The Jewish Bible today is mostly referred to as the Tanak, indicating the three parts of Jewish Scripture: Torah, Nevi'im, and Ketuvim (Law, Prophets, and Writings). Some have sought to reinvigorate the term "old" in terms of wisdom and respect. Others have changed the term to "First Testament."[1] The concern that raises for theologians of the church is that the New Testament could then be taken as the "Second Testament" and thus secondary. Another possibility is "Elder Testament."[2] I prefer the term "Older Testament" as an indication of an awareness of the terminological difficulties and an awareness that this section of the biblical canon is older and wiser and more formative than are we as interpreters. I do not believe there is a simple solution to the terminological difficulty. The phrase Old Testament theology is still the standard one in the discipline, and so I will continue to use it. I will use Old Testament and Hebrew Bible or Hebrew Scriptures interchangeably while being aware of the differences the two phrases suggest. As I have indicated, my preference is Older Testament.[3]

Another issue of terminology has to do with the parts of the Older Testament. The Hebrew canon has three parts: the Law, the Prophets, and the Writings. The Prophets include two sections: the Former Prophets (Joshua, Judges, 1–2 Samuel, and 1–2 Kings) and the Latter Prophets (Isaiah, Jeremiah, Ezekiel, and the Twelve). These two sections have a variety of connections. This book uses some terms of the Protestant organization of the canon. Chapter 4 uses the term "Historical Books" as a way to discuss the Former Prophets plus some

---

1. Goldingay, *Old Testament Theology*; McLaughlin, *Introduction to Israel's Wisdom Traditions*.
2. Seitz, *Elder Testament*.
3. The use of "Older Testament" makes clear that I interpret the text as a Christian. I am indeed a lifelong Baptist. I understand the interpretive task to be a conversation between texts and readers, guided by the shape of the text. Certainly, the context of the interpreter makes a difference, but I hope to begin with the shape of the text itself.

additional books related to the history of ancient Israel. Chapter 7 uses the heading "The Prophets" to discuss the theological perspective of the Latter Prophets. Readers will find it helpful to be aware of both sets of terminology.

This volume will focus on the theological or faith dimension of the Older Testament. That dimension relates to the sociohistorical or cultural context of these texts and to the shape and history of this literature. The hope is that readers will have prior knowledge of these areas in biblical studies. This volume will build on those areas and explore them when they relate to theological dimensions of the text. The focus here is the testimony Old Testament texts present to the divine-human engagement.

Several issues surface from time to time in this volume that merit comment. One is the connection between Old Testament theology and various critical issues tied to texts. Examples include the shape of the composition of the Pentateuch as well as the Former Prophets. Issues of composition also arise for various texts in the Latter Prophets as well. Form-critical questions are central in the study of the Psalms and Wisdom literature. Readers will bring some knowledge of these issues. Those of us reading the Older Testament theologically must interact with such historical- and literary-critical matters. I hope I have done that when needed and done it with care. It is important to address critical issues with humility, and it is important not to be controlled by them. Where these issues are clear and helpful, I have used them in the service of theological purposes. However, one must remember that the primary issue for Old Testament theologians is what the text says about God—the simple definition of "theology"—and how the text contributes to reflection on the divine-human relationship. That is the focus. Perhaps one might say that my approach is postcritical.

A second issue is the relationship of theology of the Hebrew Scriptures as treated in this volume to theological studies as pursued in contemporary theological education. The image of a two-way conversation is significant here. Theologians working today may bring theological issues, traditional theological categories, and philosophical questions into conversation with Old Testament theology as treated in this volume. Those who study the theology of the Hebrew Bible may also raise issues and categories for conversation with contemporary theologians. Such conversations can be beneficial for readers and interpreters of the Hebrew Bible and for communities of faith. At times such conversations may be difficult to follow, or to find ways forward in, but they provide possibilities for the engagement of the Hebrew canon with contemporary life and faith.

Third, what is the relationship of the theology of the Hebrew Scriptures and communities of faith, particularly with Judaism and Christianity or the church? Both Judaism and Christianity understand their faiths to fulfill the promise of the Hebrew Bible or Old Testament. Rabbinic Judaism continues to live faith as a covenant community in relationship with the creator. The proclamation of the Hebrew Scriptures nurtures that community as the community either looks forward to the fulfillment of their faith or lives currently in that fulfillment. The church is nurtured and guided by the proclamation of the Older Testament in conversation with the New Testament and the Christ event. The New Testament does not replace the Old Testament. Jesus Christ incarnates the Old Testament and, in that sense, deepens and broadens it. The New Testament understands itself to be in continuity with the Old. In some Christian communities, supersessionism, in which the New Testament takes the place of the Old, prevails in reading the Old Testament. That is unfortunate and misguided, and I seek to avoid it. I suggest rather that the Older Testament first be interpreted on its own terms as far as possible. Indeed, a full understanding of the New Testament depends on an understanding of the Old Testament, the necessary beginning for the New Testament. Christians often use the phrase "New Testament church" to refer to the church of New Testament times, but if understanding the New Testament depends on understanding the Old, then a better phrase would be "biblical church." The Old Testament proclamation speaks to the church; the Old Testament emphasizes the import of salvation by way of creator, deliverer, and prophetic word. The Hebrew Scriptures speak to both synagogue and church and are interpreted and embodied by those communities.

Fourth, what is the social location of the writer of this volume? This question is important in contemporary scholarship. I am a white male seventy-one years of age. I am a Protestant Christian and specifically a Baptist minister. I am also an academic, and part of the academic establishment, who has spent most of his life in the southern United States. I think it is inevitable that these realities have an impact on my scholarship and on my interpretation of both Scripture and Old Testament theology. At the same time, I hope I have given an honest account of the text of the Hebrew Bible and interpreted it with humility and with robust reading of its details. I seek to be aware of my assumptions. I am an ecumenical Christian and so seek to attend to various interpretations, including Jewish ones. I hope my readings of the text are candid and helpful. Interpretive communities are important. Mine include Lake Shore Baptist Church, the broader church, the guild of biblical studies, the broader academic community, and anyone who nurtures an interest in the Hebrew Bible. I understand any interpretation of the Scriptures to be incomplete. I hope this volume is a well-founded and honest effort at that task.

Many people contribute to the publication of a book. I am grateful to my graduate student colleagues, staff colleagues, faculty colleagues, and administrative colleagues at Baylor. Doctoral student Cara Forney has made a significant contribution to this volume. I heartily thank Baker Academic, especially Jim Kinney, Brandy Scritchfield, and James Korsmo.

Old Testament theology is a particularly complicated area of Old Testament studies. I hope this volume will make a meaningful contribution to the area, especially for students.

Introduction

The goal of this volume is to help students and other readers explore the faith dimension of the Older Testament in our current context by presenting a shape for Old Testament theology. How to begin and how to organize an Old Testament theology are open questions. Some contemporary scholars and readers seek a new shape for this area of study in the face of theological diversity and a current era characterized by pluralism. Several Old Testament scholars, however, suggest that in such a reality, the search for a shape for the theology of the Hebrew Scriptures is a lost cause. They argue that the search is unwise, asserting that any attempts to organize Old Testament faith in a coherent way fail in the face of the text's wide-ranging theological diversity. Such scholars often see a coherent organization as unnecessary and believe the central task at hand is to continue to interpret particular texts. Let me respond to that perspective.

I agree that we need to continue to study the theological dimensions of individual texts in the Older Testament, but I also think that contemporary readers of these texts need frameworks for such interpretive efforts. Interpretations are more fully informed when they are aware of contexts and attend to reading strategies that fit those contexts. Such careful interpretive work also helps readers to see their assumptions and to consider them critically. As I have said previously, "If we can craft a satisfying shape for Old Testament theology, it will give readers frameworks and contexts in which to read these ancient texts in beneficial ways."[1] Reading the part in light of the whole is a basic task of interpretation. This volume is my attempt to craft a satisfying shape and thus aid readers in the interpretive task.

I argue for a shape of Old Testament theology in terms of divine revelation and human response. That revelation and response has three perspectives: creation theology in which God is present to bless and offers wisdom as an avenue of response, covenant theology in which God hears and comes to deliver and shape a community in which covenant instruction provides a path for response, and prophetic theology in which YHWH speaks and calls for fidelity to the creator and liberator in response. The analogy I call on is that of three legs of a stool, a tripos. History suggests that in the old days of the University of Cambridge, students sat on a three-legged stool to be quizzed about the subjects of their undergraduate studies. I use this analogy to point to three theological perspectives at the core of the shape of revelation and response in the Older Testament. I view these three perspectives as the three legs of that stool. The question here is what constitutes the seat of the stool supported by the three legs.

My proposal for the seat of the stool is "salvation." In some faith communities, that term is located in covenant theology and tied to deliverance, and it can be defined in a variety of ways dependent on the theologies of the communities. The English word "salvation," however, derives from the Latin *salvare*, which carries a broader sense of wholeness or fullness or completeness or health. The goal of blessing, liberation, and proclamation is wholeness of life for the faith community and all in it, for creation and all in it. The Hebrew for "integrity" (*tom*, from *tmm*, as "integrity" or "wholeness"; the understanding is akin to shalom as wholeness) correlates to "salvation" in which life fits together in a holistic way in a community characterized by just and generous relationships nurtured by the creator, liberator, and guide. The diverse perspectives of the Hebrew canon support that goal. That goal reflects a loose umbrella of unity for the Hebrew canon, but any

1. Bellinger, "Shape for Old Testament Theology," 292.

step into the Hebrew text brings readers very quickly to a diversity of perspectives. Enormous diversity characterizes the Old Testament in a considerable variety of ways. In the face of that reality, I boldly propose a shape for an Old Testament Theology.

Please note that it is *a* shape and not *the* shape. At the same time, I pursue this shape in robust ways. It does not resolve the diversity of the Old Testament into a tripolar center but rather provides a heuristic avenue for organizing the theological perspectives of the Older Testament as an aid in interpretation. It presents a path that is based in the Psalms, and so begins with a textual base. It also accounts for what the text says about God and God's engagement with the world and the human community and its life. It provides a path for interested readers to pursue reading the Hebrew canon in meaningful ways. There are, no doubt, other helpful paths. My hope is that this one provides ways forward for students and other interested readers.

A Suggested Path for Shaping Old Testament Theology

As stated previously, this volume will focus on the theological or faith dimension of the Older Testament, on the testimony these texts articulate in the divine-human engagement. The faith dimension relates to the sociohistorical or cultural context of these texts and to the shape and history of this literature but emphasizes the witness to faith. Since this academic area of inquiry has a long and distinguished history in biblical studies, it stands to reason that we begin with a basic review of that history of scholarship to gather lessons from it. The discipline of Old Testament theology seeks to retain the gains of modern study of the Hebrew Scriptures while not being held captive to the extremes of modernism. For this reason, chapter 1 provides an overview of this history already hinted at in the opening discussion. As readers will no doubt notice, the current state of the discipline and its lack of direction could be paralyzing. What is central is the task of asking what God is doing in texts in the Older Testament. What does the text say about the divine-human engagement and the implications of it? How might one then begin to organize the variety of answers to such questions? In chapter 2, I suggest a textual place to begin: the book of Psalms.

The place in the Old Testament where the faith community of ancient Israel sings and confesses its faith is the central book of Psalms, ancient Israel's prayer book and hymnbook. This textual starting point both articulates the major themes of Old Testament faith and reflects the problems inherent in doing so. The book of Psalms reveals the divine side of God's engagement with all of creation and calls for human response. When we consider how God is involved with the human community, one of the two dominant psalm genres suggests that God is present to bless, to make it possible for the faithful to grow and thrive in the world. The descriptive psalms of praise illustrate that perspective well. Psalms of the other dominant genre, lament, portray YHWH as the one who hears and comes to deliver. When we consider the wider Old Testament, these two perspectives of the blessing God and the delivering God suggest the perspectives of creation theology and covenant theology. In Old Testament creation theology, God is the one who is present to bless, and the means of human response is wisdom in how to live in the creation. In Old Testament covenant theology, God is the one who hears a lament and comes to deliver, bringing about a covenant relationship, including covenant instruction or *torah*. A third perspective also surfaces in several of the psalms of praise where God is characterized as the one who speaks and calls for fidelity to the divine-human relationship. This perspective is reflected in the Latter Prophets and their calls for repentance from injustice and idolatry or from lack of faith in the divine fidelity in Israel's experience of trouble and woe. The Latter Prophets combine in complicated ways creation and covenant theological perspectives in a genre focused on divine revelation by way of prophetic voices.

At the risk of repeating, I articulate again the path we will follow. Starting with ancient Israel's liturgical confessions of faith instigates a three-part structure for articulating Old Testament faith: creation theology, in which God is present to bless, with wisdom as an avenue of response; covenant theology, in which God hears and comes to deliver, with *torah* as an avenue of response; and prophetic theology, in which God speaks and calls for fidelity from the faith community. This structuring proposal is more heuristic than determinative, and so in chapters 3–7, I will not take the three parts of the confession as a structuring device but will rather work through the parts of the canon with these three perspectives in mind to see how they are present and how they interact in shaping the Hebrew canon and a memorable portrait of salvation.

Chapter 3 attends to the formative first part of the Hebrew canon, the Torah. Appropriately, the opening book of Genesis puts creation theology on display with creation accounts and narratives of the beginnings of human experience. God here creates and blesses with the power to live and grow, and the texts teach wisdom for living in this world. The ancestral stories continue with the emphasis on the divine blessing for Abram and Sarai and their descendants as they find wisdom for living with this blessing. The language of covenant appears at times in Genesis, but the primary theological perspective is that of creation theology. In the first half of Exodus, covenant takes center stage with the faith community's cry for help in Egyptian bondage, the divine hearing of the cry, and God's coming to liberate the community. The exodus from Egypt leads to the creation of the covenant community and instruction (*torah*) in how to live in that relationship. Following the agreement of the covenant relationship, Exodus moves to instruction in worship for the faith community. The context is still covenant instruction, but the text most often functions from the perspective of creation theology in Genesis, and this emphasis continues through Leviticus and parts of Numbers. Deuteronomy concludes the Torah with powerful articulation of the covenant relationship between YHWH and Israel. The creator also provides blessing in Deuteronomy, but the focus is the gift of covenant and the call for a human response of fidelity in that relationship.

Chapter 4 begins with the Former Prophets as they continue to narrate, on the basis of Deuteronomy's covenant theology, the life of ancient Israel as the community emerges in the land of Palestine and lives its early days in the time of the judges. The covenant's hope of fidelity to that relationship does not fare well in these narratives. The result is a move to monarchy. Despite a rocky beginning, the kings are a divine gift, and especially the David narrative operates from a creation and wisdom perspective, with David as the leader of the community. The narrative of the divided kingdoms in the books of Kings recounts that era with a commentary on covenant faithfulness or unfaithfulness of the kings and the community. Chapter 4 continues with the time of exile and after, with attention to historical texts from this era and its mix of creation, covenant, and prophetic theological perspectives around themes of theodicy coming from the trauma of defeat and exile.

Chapter 5 pursues the matter of theology in the Psalms, particularly in terms of prayer and praise. The laments in Psalms bear witness to a genuine covenant interaction. Many of the hymns of praise depict the creator who rules over all creation, as do royal and wisdom psalms. In a number of psalms God also speaks about worship and about fidelity to the relationship with YHWH, an emphasis of prophetic theology. The three theological perspectives derive from the Psalms. The Psalter also relates to theodicy tied to the sixth-century-BCE defeat of Jerusalem and exile of the community.

Chapter 6 discusses wisdom traditions in the Writings. These traditions are based in creation theology. The creator placed wisdom in the world and makes it possible for the sages to learn it and pass it on so that living in line with the created order is possible. It is a means of encountering blessing. Proverbs teaches practical wisdom for living, and Job and Ecclesiastes question simplistic understandings of that wisdom around issues of undeserved suffering and the ordering of life. Daniel narrates living wisely in exile in the context of an apocalyptic hope for the completion of the reign of God.

Chapter 7 explores the prophetic theology of the Latter Prophets: Isaiah (Davidic covenant), Jeremiah (Sinaitic covenant), Ezekiel (Priestly theology), and the Twelve. The Twelve consists of a dozen parts and embraces creation and covenant theologies at various points in the context of the genre of prophecy, in which YHWH speaks messages of judgment and hope. Judgment oracles are based in injustice and idolatry in the community. Hope oracles are based in divine fidelity to the relationship with Israel reciprocated by its human partners. Prophetic oracles and prophetic books declare the divine message to the community. A number of prophetic texts indicate close connections to the Psalms and its liturgical genres. This summary suggests the import of the three legs moving toward the salvific seat of the stool labeled "Old Testament Theology."

Readerly Expectations

It is important to see that this shape for an Old Testament theology is not an attempt to cover every text and every subject in the Hebrew canon. It is rather a heuristic structure meant to give readers a context and a frame for understanding and reflecting on the text with theological categories appropriate to the text and its emphases. These three theological traditions are not separate and isolated but interact and support a full notion of salvation. They provide a framework for reading and understanding texts that reflect a noticeably different world and, for many readers, a different kind of relationship with God.

Each of the theological terms used in this tripartite shape for an Old Testament theology will carry particular connotations for various readers. For some readers, for example, "covenant" will indicate a contractual theology in which God is legally bound to deliver when *torah*, the divine instruction, is followed. Or, living by way of *torah* will be understood to be a way to guarantee deliverance. The shape of these texts in the Hebrew canon, however, makes clear that YHWH graciously delivers the community because it is in need and because of God's persistent love and fidelity to this community. Covenant has some connections to notions of contract but is not a legalistic concept. Exodus 20 begins the instruction to the people with the Decalogue, but it is crucial to see that the first commandment comes in verse 3 with the basic injunction against worshiping other gods. The benevolent history of YHWH with this people comes *prior* to the command: "I am the LORD your God, who brought you out of the land of Egypt, out of the house of slavery" (v. 2). It is not that the ancient Hebrews live in a certain way to become God's people; rather, because they *are* God's people, they are to live in a certain way characterized by the covenant instruction of *torah*. *Torah* means, most fully, covenant instruction or teaching or direction rather than law in the contractual, legal sense "law" has in contemporary language.

It is also important for readers to take care with their preconceived notions of God's deliverance. Perhaps for many readers of the Older Testament that term connotes a sudden, immediate, and miraculous escape from trouble, brought about by God. The divine power unexpectedly intervenes in history to effect human liberation. The Hebrew text clearly does include that kind of sudden rescue—at the sea in the departure from Egypt or at the collapse of Jericho. Yet deliverance is not always characterized in that way. Think about how important Moses, Aaron, and Miriam are in the exodus traditions. Remember also times when the monarchs of the ancient Hebrew kingdoms brought liberation to the people. God brings about deliverance by way of humans, and sometimes that deliverance comes in the form of a process. It is also important to remember that God enables people to persevere through crises and to come out on the other side. Perhaps Job is the quintessential example. This description may well stretch the term "deliverance" beyond recognition, but God's work to move humans from trouble to hope in ways that are not always obvious to human observers is also clearly part of the covenantal perspective in the Older Testament. The central issue here is that if readers expect God to be about the covenant business of deliverance in only one way, they may well be disappointed because of faulty assumptions. God works in a variety of ways to initiate and renew covenant relationship. This last assertion also reminds readers that the goal of this divine engagement with humans is not concluded with liberation. The focus of God's involvement is rather to cultivate a relationship embodying fullness of life, or "salvation."

"Creation" is a term that for many contemporary readers is often synonymous with "nature," but in the Hebrew Scriptures it is always essential to remember that the creator undergirds the creation and that God and humans are in relationship with the creation. This creator effects "blessing." This term is often used in contemporary colloquial language to pat a little one on the head and to keep the conversation moving ("Bless your heart"). In the Hebrew text, blessing is a powerful reality that can be placed on others by priests or leaders. Blessing comes from the presence of the creator, making it possible to carry into every day the power to grow and to thrive. The blessing of the successive generations of the ancestors had to do with the divine presence making it possible to live in hope and continue toward that hope of a full life in all its dimensions, "salvation." Wisdom as an avenue of response to that blessing is also not a matter of complying with a legalistic contract, acting rightly so that riches will come automatically. The wisdom of Proverbs is more sophisticated than that; it is in living a right and just life that one can encounter wisdom and wholeness in life. And remember that Job was a righteous man! Wisdom is the responsible living out of the creator's blessing. Such responsible living focuses not on the privilege of being blessed but on bearing witness to this blessing for all of creation and for all of humanity.

The largest concentration of "prophecy" appears in the section of the canon labeled the Latter Prophets. Prophecy is about the future, but it is not fortune-telling for the distant future. It is rather proclamation of what God is preparing to do in the hearing community's future, tied to the nature of the audience's relationship with God. It is this kind of foretelling, and it is forth-telling—proclamation of a word from God. The prophets were characterized as messengers, carrying a message from YHWH to the people of ancient Israel. It is important to emphasize that the message is of divine origin and that the prophet embodies the message. The prophet is central in the shaping of this urgent divine revelation. Through the prophet YHWH speaks. The anticipated avenue of response to this proclamation is repentance. The most common Hebrew word used is *shuv*, meaning "to turn around." The experience of a friend of mine illustrates the image of repentance. My friend walked to work (to a church!) through a rough neighborhood and had done so for several years. One day someone who appeared to be a homeless person collapsed to the ground near her. Some companions gathered around. My friend thought, "I will go to the other side of the street and avoid this crisis so I can get to work on time." As she crossed the street, she realized that was the wrong direction, turned around to help the person who had collapsed, and called emergency personnel. She repented, turned to a different path. Likewise, the hearing community or person is walking a path of faithlessness, injustice, unrighteousness, and evil that brings death. To repent is a conscious stopping and turning around to walk in the direction of faith, justice, righteousness, and hope and to encounter fullness of life, "salvation." The specifics of the divine message and of the response are tied to the context of the prophecy. The messages are renewals of creation and covenant dimensions of the divine-human relationship tied to needs of the current sociohistorical context, and in a distinct literary guise. In that sense, the prophets were preachers of righteousness. Their proclamations demonstrate the divine pathos toward the faith community in a considerable variety of settings with the hope of speaking in turn to all of creation and humanity.

Hermeneutics

Up to this point, the proposed shape for an Old Testament theology has attended to categories and definitions appropriate to the theological dimensions of the Older Testament so as to organize a theology that embraces the diverse forms and themes constituting the Hebrew canon. The Psalms provides a fruitful place to begin. It will now be important to reflect more broadly on the methodology employed.

The central form of the Psalms in terms of prayer and praise suggests that the theological dimensions are tied to divine engagement with creation and its creatures. At least in its initial stages this engagement begins with divine initiative. YHWH is revealed in blessing, delivering, and speaking; creation, covenant, and prophecy begin on the divine side of the relationship. Thus, I follow the pattern of revelation and response. These categories align well with the understanding that theology is a word about God and thus about revelation and its implications. Wisdom, *torah*, and repentance are about response to the divine. We will see as we move further into the texts that the reality of this relational way of thinking is more complicated, but these categories of revelation and response are true to the text and provide a fruitful heuristic organizing pattern.[2] They reflect the relational character of the Older Testament's theological dimensions. Hermeneutics is about the art of interpretation, and the categories used are defining in interpretive work. The categories of revelation and response fit the Old Testament context.

Another hermeneutical pattern involved in this proposal is that work on the theological perspectives of the Older Testament begins with the Hebrew text, as reflected in the textual starting place of the Psalms, and so considers the initiating cultural contexts of the various textual traditions. Theological interpretation centers on the conversation between texts and readers informed by the cultural codes imbedded in texts. So it is important that theological work on the Older Testament is not captured by the ancient in limiting ways. In this work these ancient texts are in conversation with reading communities and thus with contemporary life. That is fundamental to the theological task and inherent to the task of theological interpretation of the Hebrew Scriptures.[3] Attending to both the ancient text and the contemporary context is a complicated task. The best practice is the goal of dynamic analogy. Theological interpretation needs to articulate carefully the analogy between an ancient text within its settings and contemporary contexts; that task requires both care and imagination. The analogy needs to be sufficiently dynamic to make the moves from the ancient through history to the contemporary. This project will be heavy on the textual shape and context but with an eye to the contemporary

2. John Kessler uses divine call and human response in structuring his *Old Testament Theology*, and Walther Zimmerli structures his *Old Testament Theology in Outline* in terms of revelation and response in contexts of crisis and hope.

3. Clements, *Old Testament Theology*, 191–99.

reading community of faith. So how might we proceed with the notion of dynamic analogy?

One important part of the picture is that the Hebrew Scriptures greatly value narrative as a means of communicating a word about God. Narrative is the primary genre of the Older Testament. In Genesis, the primeval history and the ancestral narratives make considerable use of that form. The first half of Exodus narrates the liberation from Egypt. Legal forms dominate the latter portion of Exodus and continue through Leviticus and on into the first part of Numbers, though recent studies of law suggest connections with narrative.[4] While there are some other genres in the Former Prophets, narrative is the primary means of recounting this portion of ancient Israel's history from emerging in the land of Canaan to the fall of Jerusalem to the Babylonians in the sixth century BCE. The later historical works of 1–2 Chronicles, Ezra, and Nehemiah make considerable use of the form. Ruth and Esther, in the Writings section of the Hebrew canon, are also narratives, and the distinctive book of the prophet Jonah is narrative in form. Perhaps the story of this prophet illustrates the movement of dynamic analogy. Jonah is a character given a divine message, and that message confronts him with the reality that the creator's grace is not limited to the elect Israel but could even extend to the archenemy Assyria. Most interpreters understand the prophetic character to be representative of Second Temple Judaism. The dynamic analogy extends to communities of faith that through history and even today confront the theological reality that divine grace is central to any conversation about particularist or universalist tendencies in theological understandings. This example illustrates the reception of the significance of narrative. All people live a story. That is the form of human living, and so narrative texts relate to narrative lives. The form of narration of theological perspectives

---

4. See Bartor, *Reading Law as Narrative*; Halberstam, "Art of Biblical Law"; Milgrom, "Law and Narrative and the Exegesis of Leviticus XIX 19"; Barmash, "Narrative Quandary"; Nasuti, "Identity, Identification, and Imitation." From the perspective of legal studies: Brooks, "Narrativity of the Law"; Cover, "Nomos and Narrative"; Ward, *Law and Literature*; West, *Narrative, Authority, and Law*.

from the Old Testament is a particularly apt way to tie the text to contemporary life. Theological interpretation of texts in the Hebrew Bible needs to attend to the narrative context and analogous human narratives. So attention to the narrative form is important in relating Old Testament theology to contemporary life.

Not all of the Older Testament, however, is in the form of narrative. The Psalms and Wisdom literature, along with Lamentations and Song of Songs and most of the Latter Prophets, are in poetic form. Yet recent scholarship on the Psalms has tellingly pursued the "narrative impulse" in the poetry of the Psalter,[5] and even Proverbs and Job include narrative scenes. This interpretive move supports the importance of narrative in communicating theological content. These texts are not in the genre of story or narrative, but they are dramatic in effect. They assume a dramatic context, whether it be the dialogue of Job or the Song, the divine-human dialogue of the Psalter, or the divine address of the community in the Prophets. That is why these texts are so amenable to analogies with lived experience of communities and persons in other times and places.

Still, the poetic language of such texts makes its contribution. Poetic forms become part of our collective memories. Because of their force and form, poetic lines and stanzas stay with us and become the means of our interpreting experience in theological ways and in terms of the divine-human relationship. The poetry itself is part of the framework for living that persons carry through life and instructs people in how to live as part of a just community of faith, how to pray, how to worship, how to come to terms with the troubling issues of theodicy so present in contemporary life and thought. So Old Testament texts in both narrative and poetic forms shape memory for contemporary communities and readers. The narratives and poetry become parts of the frameworks readers carry in their collective memories and shape their perspectives, their attitudes, and their lives.

The legal materials in the Hebrew Bible operate in a similar way. They become life-structuring warnings and invitations to live in ways

5. See Alter, *Art of Biblical Poetry*.

commensurate with covenant relationships. The forms are somewhat different, but the function is similar to that of prophetic warnings. These texts become formative for curated memory for those living in right relationship with God and with neighbor. These psychological, sociological, and linguistic memories shape the frameworks that construct life for humans. These cognitive frameworks may well manifest themselves in ethical contexts or in intellectual pursuits on the pressing questions of human life and meaning. They consider the basic human condition, the search for hope, the structuring of life and community, and how God relates to those basic issues. Narrative, memory, and cognitive frames are central to the connection of Old Testament theology to contemporary life.

It is appropriate to speak of entering the narrative of the text and encountering its significance and living in its world. It is also appropriate to speak of appropriating the narrative as a part of life and embodying the narrative. Much of this volume articulates a narrative approach to Old Testament theology. Narrating the plot of the text with an emphasis on the divine encounter therein is central to the task of Old Testament theology. It is in lived reality that readers encounter the theological import of texts. Such narratives form life. The court prophet Nathan understands this when he tells King David the story, the narrative, of the rich man taking the poor man's ewe lamb. David sees immediately the sin and realizes that he, David, has done just that with Bathsheba. David enters the narrative world of the story—that is, he incorporates the narrative into his life. In just such a way, contemporary readers and reading communities can engage the narrative that communicates the theology of the Hebrew Scriptures, the focus of which is the divine-human encounter.

Imagery is another powerful literary means of engaging the human imagination, and the imagination makes it possible to embrace the imagery, to experience its significance, and to embody it. Such imagery becomes part of the memory readers carry with them and embody in life. The image beginning book 2 of the Hebrew Psalter (Ps. 42), of a doe needing water to live, communicates powerfully by analogy the human need for the divine presence. Isaiah's characterization of Israel as a vineyard shapes the human imagination in ways that have an impact on readers and interpretive communities. Such images and narratives, which pervade the Older Testament, can become part of the memory readers and communities carry with them through the narrative of life as a script for living in faith. Memory focuses both the present and the future. Prophetic proclamations of hope and critiques of injustice and infidelity carried in memory can alter the course of life. Memories of narratives of liberation can inspire acts of liberation. The call of Woman Wisdom at the highways and byways of life can bring reflection on the order of life. Such memories shape life. The discipline of psychology includes the psychology of personal constructs.[6] That is, people view reality through constructs that guide the perception and interpretation of experience. For example, the Psalter's affirmation of God as creator can become part of our own perspective and how we relate to the created order. The prophetic calls for justice can become a central construct in shaping our human relationships. These constructs become part of our memory, shaping how we live and how we view life. And we test these constructs in our experience. These constructs can lead to the social construction of reality and to important questions about power and social location involved in our hermeneutical work on the Older Testament. By way of these constructs, these ancient texts may wield authority in liturgical communities. Narrative and memory are central in the appropriation of Old Testament theology in the life of faith.

Another connection has to do with the context of the reading community. This volume begins with the Psalms, the ancient faith community's cultic literature. The liturgical context of these texts that confess ancient Israel's faith is important. These texts are ancient Israel's pilgrimage songs of faith. The community sang these songs as confessions of their faith as a means of forming and renewing their faithful memories and imaginations, so that they might embody the

6. Kelly, *Theory of Personality*; Neimeyer and Neimeyer, *Personal Construct Therapy Casebook*, 3–19.

narrative of faith on the journey through life as well as the courage
and care needed to continue on this journey. One of the implications
of this viewpoint is that the most effective context for forming such
communities of faith is a liturgical context—that is, a worshiping community. A worshiping community best shapes and holds accountable
readers and communities for the encounter with theological perspectives in the Hebrew Scriptures. Such a community shaped the narrative
and poetry of the Older Testament, and such a community today can
best receive this kind of theological memoir so that its imagination is
shaped for living this memory. "Scott Momaday of the University of
Southern California has told how his father took him as a child to spend
a day with an older Kiowa woman to hear and participate in the story,
ritual, and song of his people. He says he left that woman's house a
Kiowa."[7] Just in this sense, immersion in the Psalter begins and fulfills
the hopes of Old Testament theology. "Narratives function to sustain
the particular moral identity of a religious (or secular) community by
rehearsing its history and traditional meanings, as these are portrayed
in Scripture and other sources. . . . Through our participation in such
a community, the narratives also function to give shape to our moral
characters, which in turn deeply affect the way we interpret or construe
the world and events and thus affect what we determine to be appropriate action as members of the community."[8] Narratologists argue that
stories can impact our lives and shape our character.

The purpose of this volume is not to articulate all the theological
dimensions of the Older Testament but to prepare students and other
readers to productively ask theological questions when interpreting
Old Testament texts: What is God doing in this text? What characterizes the divine encounter with creation? What are the implications of
the divine-human encounter in the text? The study of historical and
historical-critical issues and languages in the academic study of the
Hebrew Scriptures can easily diminish the theological questions. And
yet the theological questions are at the heart of the purpose of the

7. Bellinger, "Psalms as a Place to Begin for Old Testament Theology," 36.
8. Gustafson, "Varieties of Moral Discourse," 56.

text for both ancient and contemporary reading communities. The shape proposed for Old Testament theology in this volume provides a context for this interpretive work. The accounts of the parts of the Hebrew canon in chapters 3–7 articulate background for theological work on these texts. The hope is that this introductory account of Old Testament theology will encourage and help in the task of reading the Older Testament theologically. Such reading is life changing.

1

Beginnings

For many people, the Old Testament or Hebrew Bible is a terribly neglected, even lost, source of faith. Brent Strawn has suggested that the Old Testament is dying, much like a language might, and he proposes ways to reinvigorate it as an authority for life and faith.[1] This volume likewise seeks to provide a basis for reading this Hebrew text as a powerful document and for studying it from theological perspectives.

The theological study of the Older Testament has a long tradition in the history of Christian theology and, differently, in Judaism. This history is a gift, and from it contemporary readers and students can learn a great deal about approaches used in the theological study of these texts and about the theological import of particular texts. There is a sense in which this history of scholarship forms a narrative that contemporary readers can enter and participate in as part of the story of Old Testament theology. It is important to recount that narrative so that all of us, author and readers alike, can take our place in that story. Our current entry into the story comes at a time of fraught opportunity for readers of these texts. While a number of publications

1. See Strawn, *Old Testament Is Dying*.

have recently contributed to the theological study of the Older Testament, the judgment of Walter Brueggemann from 1985 still holds
true: "The organization of an Old Testament theology is clearly now
a quite open and unresolved question. The comprehensive designs of
Walther Eichrodt and Gerhard von Rad are now found wanting and
we must find a new shape."[2] Finding a way forward is important for
a number of reasons.

The Bible relates to theological matters in a variety of ways, and
the Older Testament is most of the Bible. Most Christian and Jewish
readers come to these texts primarily for reasons related to faith or
theology. The organization chosen for such theological reflection is no
small matter and requires the use of all the resources at hand. A central
resource is the story of the discipline of Old Testament theology.

The story has its beginnings even in the canonical texts themselves.[3]
For example, Psalm 8 reflects on the creation account in Genesis 1,
and Job 3 and 7 reflect on Genesis 1 and Psalm 8, respectively. The
Hebrew prophetic corpus also often reflects on theological traditions
in ancient Israel. Rabbis did the same in ways central to the shaping of
rabbinic Judaism. Turning to the New Testament, Matthew begins by
putting the story of Jesus in the context of narratives from the Older
Testament. Speeches in Acts often quote Psalms, and Paul frequently
refers to texts from the Jewish Scriptures. The task of theological reflection on the Hebrew Scriptures has been part of the Judeo-Christian
tradition for millennia. Today's readers can learn much from that
story.

The story continues in the early centuries of the Christian church
with theologians using texts from the Older Testament to support
the practices of the church in Rome. By contrast, theologians such as
Martin Luther and John Calvin often used the same texts to attack the
practices of the church in Rome. Such prooftexting has been a common approach to the Older Testament throughout the history of the
church.

2. Brueggemann, "Shape for Old Testament Theology, 1," 28.
3. See Fishbane, *Biblical Interpretation in Ancient Israel.*

The Move to Modernity

Interpretation of the Hebrew Scriptures has a long history, but biblical theology as an area of academic study developed after the various reformations of the sixteenth century and so was an invention of modernity.[4] With the coming of the Enlightenment in the eighteenth century and its emphases on reason and history, theologians began to move more explicitly toward questions of hermeneutics, the art of interpretation, and clarity about the differences between the Older Testament and the New Testament. J. S. Semler, for example, emphasized the historical-critical approach to biblical texts, arguing that the canon is a historical volume and should be investigated as such.[5] Shortly afterwards came an important beginning point of the discipline: Johann Philipp Gabler's 1787 lecture "A Discourse on the Proper Distinction between Biblical and Dogmatic Theology and the Correct Delimitation of Their Boundaries."[6] As indicated above, the Bible had been studied for centuries as part of the Christian church. That is, the Bible was studied in an ecclesial framework: "The purpose of biblical study was to support doctrines of the church, i.e., dogmatic theology. Gabler asserts the independence of biblical theology from dogmatics. His approach is an historical one seeking what the various biblical authors said in their historical setting. Once the tenets of biblical theology were in place, one could apply them to church doctrine."[7]

Childs notes that "the emancipation of the discipline from its dependency on ecclesiastical doctrine" has continued as a central tenet of Old Testament theology.[8] Additional works in the area continued to appear with various approaches. Toward the end of the eighteenth century, however, the trend to separate Old Testament theology and New Testament theology had come to the fore.[9] The traditional organization

4. Childs, *Biblical Theology*, 107.
5. Semler, *Abhandlung von freier Untersuchung des Kanon.*
6. Sandys-Wunsch and Eldridge, "J. P. Gabler and the Distinction between Biblical and Dogmatic Theology."
7. Bellinger, "Shape for Old Testament Theology," 287.
8. Childs, *Biblical Theology*, 5–6.
9. Bauer, *Theologie des Alten Testaments.*

of Old Testament theology into divisions of theology, anthropology, and Christology also appeared in Bauer's work. In line with broader intellectual movements, the emphasis on the history of religions came to dominate in the nineteenth century. The interest was not in theological reflection on the Hebrew Scriptures but in the evolutionary, historical development of ancient Israel's religion. The works of Julius Wellhausen provide the most familiar example.[10] The history of religions approach is an important part of the background of the flowering of Old Testament theology.

The Era of Eichrodt and von Rad

Every story has its heroes, and the first major character in the story of Old Testament theology is the Swiss theologian Walther Eichrodt.[11] His volumes appeared in German in the 1930s. Eichrodt reasserted the importance of the theological perspective of the text while taking into account the historical contribution that was so important in the work of those who studied the Older Testament. He also gave space to questions of the Hebrew Scriptures' relationship to the New Testament and the church. Questions of method were also central to Eichrodt's work. He suggests a way forward in which readers take a "cross-section" of the dynamic faith developed in the Older Testament "in order to explore the Old Testament's structure of belief."[12] The analogy of a cross-section is that of a logger who removes a core

10. Contemporary biblical criticism owes much of its vitality to the pioneering work of Wellhausen. In 1882 he proposed a sharp transition in the course of Israel's religious history. Israel's early religious conceptions looked much like those of their ancient neighbors. For example, Wellhausen notes similarities between the people of YHWH and the people of Chemosh regarding ideas of a warlike patron god as the head of the nation. A major shift occurred when the eighth-century prophets sought to sweep away "the old popular half-pagan conception of Jehovah" and thus laid the groundwork for Deuteronomic theology. Wellhausen, *Prolegomena to the History of Israel*, 491. For more on Wellhausen's work and its impact, see Hahn, "Wellhausen's Interpretation of Israel's Religious History," 299–308; Hayes, "Wellhausen as a Historian of Israel," 37–60; Childs, "Wellhausen in English"; Clements, *Century of Old Testament Study*, esp. 7–12.

11. Eichrodt, *Theology of the Old Testament*.

12. Anderson, *Contours of Old Testament Theology*, 19.

sample from a tree to obtain a small cross-section showing the rings of the tree and the development of its growth. Just so, a scholar can take a cross-section of the Old Testament at some point and learn the shape and development of the faith of ancient Israel. Eichrodt thus asserts that there is a unity to the faith of this ancient community in its various eras. His approach, then, is a synchronic one—that is, he understands the faith the Old Testament commends as structurally consistent through time. He goes a step further in arguing that when readers look at the cross-section of Old Testament faith, the structure that is consistently visible is a covenant structure emphasizing the re- lationship between God and people. The two crucial proposals from Eichrodt thus are that one ought to begin by taking a cross-section of Hebrew faith and that when one examines the cross-section, one finds the center of that faith in covenant. He then organizes his theological work systematically in three parts: God and Israel, God and the world, and God and humanity. He is clear that he is selecting and organizing this theological work but seeks to do so from the inside of the faith the Old Testament asserts. His work began a major effort to find the center of Old Testament faith—in German, *die Mitte*.

Eichrodt's massive work brought a rebirth to the academic study of Old Testament theology. To the fore of this study came questions of method tied to the question of whether Old Testament faith has a center and whether proposed centers adequately account for the considerable diversity in the Older Testament. Eichrodt's proposal of covenant as the center raised the same issue. Questions of the rela- tionship between particularism and universalism became important in this conversation. The rich diversity of theological perspectives in the Hebrew Scriptures and whether there is a unifying theme for them continue to raise significant questions for Old Testament theologians.

Eichrodt's formative work initiated what has been called the golden age of Old Testament theology.[13] Method was central to this work,

13. Hasel, *Old Testament Theology*, 26; see also his chapter on the search for a center of Old Testament faith.

and scholars proposed various centers for Old Testament faith. It will be helpful to note some representative works to see the variety of approaches, methods, and proposals. Ludwig Köhler's 1936 *Old Testament Theology* proposed the lordship of God as the center and organized the theology around God, anthropology, and judgment and salvation. Köhler emphasized that the Old Testament does not synthesize its theological reflection; the scholar does that. He understood the task to be to articulate the thought of the Old Testament. Theodorus Vriezen in 1949 offered another relational proposal, communion, as *die Mitte* for Old Testament faith.[14] His attempt was also confessional, expositing the normative faith of ancient Israel. Edmond Jacob's 1955 volume proposed a descriptive approach, viewing the task as historical in nature.[15] His helpful volume represents the systematized style of presentation which was common in the middle of the twentieth century. Walther Zimmerli published his work in 1972.[16] He begins with the self-revelation formula "I am YHWH," emphasizing its place at the head of the Decalogue. Because theology is a word about God, he thus organizes the work around revelation and response in settings of crisis and hope.

As suggested in the quote from Brueggemann early in this chapter, the second major character in the narrative of Old Testament theology is German theologian Gerhard von Rad. Von Rad continues the emphasis on method, but he also emphasizes the diversity of Old Testament faith traditions.[17] He writes about the *theologies* of the Old Testament and suggests that the best approach is to trace those various theological traditions. He attends, for example, to the theological perspectives of the various sources in the Pentateuch, to the perspectives from which the histories of the divided kingdoms arise, and to the emphases of each prophetic figure. His approach is thus diachronic in contrast to Eichrodt's synchronic approach. The two volumes of von Rad's *Old Testament Theology* are titled *The Theology of Israel's Historical*

14. Vriezen, *Outline of Old Testament Theology.*
15. Jacob, *Theology of the Old Testament.*
16. Zimmerli, *Old Testament Theology in Outline.*
17. Von Rad, *Old Testament Theology.*

Traditions and *The Theology of Israel's Prophetic Traditions.* As these titles suggest, von Rad's work is often characterized as a history of traditions approach, but I would suggest there is more to his methodology. Von Rad seeks the early oral expression of ancient Israel's faith, and he explores the character of those early, brief confessions of faith. Out of those brief confessions grew the historical faith articulated in the Hebrew Bible. Deuteronomy 26:5–10 is a prime example of such a historical credo; it begins with the ancestral promise and continues through the exodus and settlement in the land of Canaan. In von Rad's view, the Older Testament tells that story again and again through the generations, expanding into what became ancient Israel's history of salvation. The second volume traces how the prophets connected the traditions of the faith for their historical settings; the prophets spoke the faith again for their generations. For von Rad, there is no one idea at the center; rather, there are retellings of the history of YHWH with the community of ancient Israel. He remains interested in the relationship of these traditions to worship and to the New Testament. The questions his work raises are rather different from those Eichrodt's work raised. Now the questions become whether this approach carries too much diversity, and indeed whether methodological issues have become too important. Is von Rad's work more a history of ancient Israel's traditions than an Old Testament theology? In a sense, von Rad has proposed a different center of the salvation history of ancient Israel, especially in the tradition of Deuteronomy. Von Rad is also often criticized for giving little attention to the Psalms and Wisdom literature. These texts don't seem to fit his salvation history pattern. He classifies them as Israel's response to that history. These critiques are substantial, but von Rad's contributions to the narrative of Old Testament theology are enormous and lasting.

Von Rad's emphasis on history is related to developments in the United States that have been titled "the biblical theology movement." A number of American Old Testament scholars in the middle of the twentieth century were optimistic about what they could discover about the history of ancient Israel—especially with the tool of archaeology—and about the possibility that through that process, they could discover the distinct divine revelation through history that is recorded in the Old Testament. The God who acts in history features in the theological works of George Ernest Wright, John Bright, and W. F. Albright, the leaders of the biblical theology movement.[18] This approach was a dominant one in the Anglo-American world in the middle of the last century. Serious issues began to surface with this historical approach in the 1960s, and indeed with the approaches of Eichrodt and von Rad. Von Rad had actually initiated some of the difficulty by articulating a sharp difference between the history of ancient Israel and the historical traditions preserved in the Hebrew Scriptures. As work continued in history and archaeology, the risk became clear in basing an Old Testament theology on a simple and direct connection with ancient Israel's history.

The Latter Part of the Twentieth Century

In 1970, the American scholar Brevard Childs published *Biblical Theology in Crisis* and pronounced the death of the biblical theology movement. For Childs, the historical critics had failed in their purpose of providing a basis for a biblical theology. He also argues that even if they had been successful, they would have imprisoned biblical faith in an ancient past and hidden it from contemporary communities of faith. That result is very odd for a literature that has formed communities of faith for centuries. Childs argues for an emphasis on the Christian canon as the context for theological reflection as the way forward. So in this proposal, he moves away from ancient history and historical-critical work toward the final form of the text itself as the basis for theological reflection. His perspective has raised many questions and brought many contributions. Some of the questions are crucial to the task of the theological study of the Older Testament. There is no single canon for the Old Testament or for the Christian Bible. Canons vary with communities of faith. Which one is to be

---

18. Wright, *God Who Acts*; Bright, *Authority of the Old Testament*; Albright, *From the Stone Age to Christianity*.

the canonical basis for theological reflection? In *Biblical Theology in Crisis*, Childs emphasizes the Christian canon and so the connection of the Older Testament with the New Testament. In other works, he explores other dimensions of canon: the literary shape of canonical books, reception history of canonical texts, the various canonical perspectives on traditional Old Testament themes.[19] Some worry that Childs's connection of the canon to the church puts at risk the hardwon independence of biblical theology from dogmatic theology. This concern is a serious matter. At the same time, Childs's emphasis on the final, canonical form of the text as the context for theological reflection profoundly influenced Old Testament theology in the last decades of the twentieth century, thus earning him the place as the third major character in this narrative.

Other scholars also explored issues related to canon. James Sanders's work is often compared to Childs's. Sanders emphasizes the hermeneutical dimensions of canon formation more than the final canonical form of the text.[20] Ronald Clements also explores the development of the canon.[21] The more recent volume by Rolf Rendtorff also attends to canonical issues.[22] In the German context, he pursues many of the issues raised by Childs with an additional interest in the Jewish reception of the Hebrew Scriptures.

Contrasting with Childs's canonical approach are sociological readings of the Hebrew Scriptures. Norman Gottwald is a leading voice in this approach.[23] He understands the Hebrew recounting of history as arising from social conflict and struggle. He considers these origins crucial for grasping its theological implications. One might suggest that Childs understands the text as speaking from above with divine revelation and Gottwald understands the message as arising from below in the human struggle for liberation. The well-recognized work of Erhard

19. See especially Childs, *Exodus*; Childs, *Introduction to the Old Testament as Scripture*; and Childs, *Old Testament Theology in a Canonical Context*.
20. Sanders, *Torah and Canon*; Sanders, "Adaptable for Life," 531–60.
21. Clements, *Old Testament Theology*.
22. Rendtorff, *Canonical Hebrew Bible*. See also Rendtorff's *Canon and Theology*.
23. Gottwald, *Tribes of Yahweh*.

Gerstenberger also fits here.[24] Gerstenberger clearly follows in the path of those who emphasize the theological diversity in the Older Testament. He interprets the texts in terms of the social settings from which they derive and so articulates theologies of villages, cities, and nations, for example. These interpretations in a sociological vein correspond to contemporary liberation theologies.

Another trend in the 1970s and 1980s has been labeled bipolar theologies. The primary assertion is that there is not one center for Old Testament theology; rather, two robust themes interact with each other in creative tension. For Claus Westermann, many of the historical texts in the Old Testament bear witness to the God who comes to deliver and call the people into covenant relationship. Additionally, a number of creation texts bear witness to the God who blesses the community in creation and calls them to life in that context.[25] The relationship between history/deliverance and creation/blessing texts is important for grasping the theological perspectives of the Old Testament. Samuel Terrien's *The Elusive Presence* articulates an ethical/aesthetic polarity; both are significant in the Hebrew texts' characterization of the divine. Paul Hanson speaks of creative tension between the cosmic and the teleological in Old Testament texts.[26] These are but examples of works that suggest two poles of theological perspective in constructive relationship in the Old Testament.[27] Prior to these works, the historical, ethical, teleological perspectives have been vastly dominant in the interpretive tradition. Such an imbalance unjustly flattens the various theological perspectives at tension within the texts. In some ways, this issue goes all the way back to the work of Eichrodt and his attention to both particularism and universalism in Old Testament theology.

This trend to consider both history/deliverance and creation/blessing (to use Westermann's categories) as poles representing important dimensions of the structures of Old Testament theology relates to a

24. Gerstenberger, *Theologies in the Old Testament*.
25. Westermann, *Blessing in the Bible and the Life of the Church*; Westermann, *What Does the Old Testament Say about God?*
26. Hanson, *Dynamic Transcendence*.
27. Brueggemann, "Convergence in Recent Old Testament Theologies."

renewed emphasis on creation as having a central importance for the Old Testament. For most of the twentieth century, the emphasis in Old Testament study has been in the direction of historical texts and covenant. Von Rad, in particular, maintained that creation was secondary to the exodus traditions and a rather late entrant to significant theological themes in the Hebrew Scriptures. Ancient Israel's theologians reasoned back from God's creation of a people through the exodus to God's creation of the world, perhaps in the face of Canaanite nature religions' claims of fertility in creation.[28] H. H. Schmid's work is significant in a change of scholarly direction in the latter half of the twentieth century.[29] He suggests that creation may be the structural center for the faith of the Old Testament. In this perspective, covenant originates from a background of creation and seeks to renew the order of creation. Rolf Knierim has also pursued these issues.[30] Perhaps the most complete statement of the importance of creation in Old Testament faith is Terence Fretheim's volume *God and World in the Old Testament*. He reviews how creation relates to the various parts of the Hebrew Scriptures. These studies seek to redress the imbalance resulting from the dominance of work on history and covenant in the structures of Old Testament faith. Some would subsume covenant under the theme of creation, but the way forward most faithful to Old Testament texts is to see the two themes in conversation with each other.

Leo Perdue has done a great service in chronicling the movements in the discipline of Old Testament theology in the latter part of the twentieth century and the beginning of the twenty-first. His two volumes *The Collapse of History* and *Reconstructing Old Testament Theology* provide insightful commentary on the current state of this area of academic study.[31] Perdue chronicles the shift away from history as the basis for theological reflection on the Older Testament, in part for reasons suggested in this chapter. Questions about the history of

28. Von Rad, *Old Testament Theology*.
29. H. Schmid, "Creation, Righteousness, and Salvation."
30. Knierim, *Task of Old Testament Theology*.
31. Barr, *Concept of Biblical Theology*, also reviews the broad history of Old Testament theology issues in the twentieth century.

ancient Israel, about how much of that history is available to contemporary interpreters, and about historical-critical work and methods are central to that important shift. But a move to postmodernity's pluralism is also central. Theological reflection on the Older Testament has traditionally sought to organize the faith of the Old Testament in a unifying way. By the end of the twentieth century, that task seemed impossible. The new emphasis was on the diversity of the Hebrew Scriptures. Perdue notes three central developments to that end. First, feminists have articulated ways the Hebrew Scriptures relate to the lives of women;[32] second, narratologists have studied Hebrew narrative and its theological implications;[33] third, metaphorical theologies have imagined new ways to articulate theological perspectives in the Hebrew Bible. Crucial issues about human imagination and hermeneutics relate to this third development. Walter Brueggemann's volume, summarized below, illustrates metaphorical theologies. Pluralism rules the day.

In Perdue's second volume, he traces further developments of differing perspectives, including African American contributions, womanist theological perspectives, and Jewish contributions. African American and womanist (African American feminist) interpreters work from a liberation theology vantage point.[34] Jewish contributions are also more present with the work of Marc Brettler, Michael Fishbane, Jon Levenson, and Marvin Sweeney.[35] Perdue illustrates the diversity of the theological and academic world and its impact on the theological task in Old Testament studies: "By the time one arrives at the conclusion of Perdue's two volumes, it has become clear that the image he borrows from theologian Lonnie Kliever is most appropriate, namely, a

32. See Trible, *God and the Rhetoric of Sexuality*; Trible, *Texts of Terror*; Dempsey, *Prophets*; Dempsey, *Hope amid the Ruins*; Dempsey, *Earth, Wind, and Fire*; Dempsey, "'Whore' of Ezekiel 16."

33. Robert Alter's *Art of Biblical Narrative* is the best-known example. John Goldingay's *Old Testament Theology* also reflects this trend.

34. See Felder, *Stony the Road We Trod*; Bailey, *Yet with a Steady Beat*; and, on the latter prophets and theology from a womanist view, Weems, *Battered Love*.

35. See, for example, Brettler, "Jewish Theology of the Psalms"; Brettler, "Jewish Approach to Psalm 111"; Fishbane, *Sacred Attunement*; Fishbane, *Exegetical Imagination*; Levenson, "Why Jews Are Not Interested in Biblical Theology"; Levenson, *Creation and the Persistence of Evil*; Levenson, *Resurrection and the Restoration of Israel*; Sweeney, "Why Jews Are Interested in Biblical Theology"; Sweeney, *Reading the Hebrew Bible after the Shoah*; Sweeney, *Tanak*.

'shattered spectrum.' Those engaging in theological reflection on the Hebrew Bible are many and extremely varied. Pluralism is the order of the day. The attempt to organize an Old Testament theology does look like a lost cause."[36]

The celebrated example that is an exception to Perdue's conclusion is the influential work of Walter Brueggemann. In 1997 Brueggemann published his *Theology of the Old Testament*; it has been characterized both as a metaphorical theology in Perdue's terms and as the first postmodern Old Testament theology. Recent developments in the area of Old Testament theology have come to the view that one center is not sufficient to organize such a constructive effort. One rubric cannot include the considerable diversity of Old Testament faith. Brueggemann has been a significant figure in noting the diversity and tensions in the Old Testament's faith expressions. In his formative and creative theology, he uses the metaphor of the courtroom to articulate the diverse faith. With this image, Brueggemann explores ancient Israel's core testimony to YHWH their God, then counter testimony, unsolicited testimony, and embodied testimony. The image of the courtroom makes it possible for Brueggemann to articulate the diversity of faith. He understands that there are limits to the metaphor, but this lengthy and comprehensive volume is a remarkable achievement in the cultural and academic context near the end of the twentieth century. Not surprisingly, while Brueggemann clearly strives to attend to the diversity of faith expressions in the Old Testament, he is primarily a covenant theologian who understands liberation theology as central to covenant. He does attend to the theme of creation in the Hebrew Scriptures, in line with recent Old Testament studies noted above, but creation is not at the center of his theology. Brueggemann's basic image of the courtroom could unfortunately be used by some to interpret the Old Testament in legalistic ways. Still, this volume is a robust example of scholarship that works to deal with the tensions in the Older Testament's revelation of the divine. He certainly deserves the label as the fourth major character in this history of scholarship.

36. Bellinger, "Shape for Old Testament Theology," 290.

It is clear that Eichrodt, von Rad, Childs, and Brueggemann—four white male Protestants—have not solved the various riddles that face theologians of the Older Testament. The history of scholarship I have reviewed is a gift and lays important groundwork while raising many questions. We still search for a path forward. The quote from Brueggemann in the introduction to this chapter still holds: how one organizes an Old Testament theology remains an open and unresolved question. Most interpreters would agree that Perdue's image of a "shattered spectrum" is particularly appropriate for our current context with pluralism at the fore. Perdue's work also demonstrates that in this discipline women, people of color, and scholars of various faith traditions now make essential contributions to this rich tapestry of explorations of faith in the Older Testament. Indeed, some of my colleagues who study the Old Testament / Hebrew Bible would suggest that the search to organize an Old Testament theology is a lost cause. The faith of this book is too diverse to organize in any meaningful way, and why would we bother? We do not need to organize such a theology but rather need to continue to work at interpreting individual texts and attending to theological themes that arise in that task. So while the history of scholarship recounted above is intended to portray some coherence for the field, even this review reveals a striking plurality of approaches and themes. It's complicated! So why continue on this path?

It is important that we continue to work at the theological interpretation of individual Hebrew biblical texts, but is that sufficient? The question I raise is, What do we give up when we decide not to attempt to organize such work into a recognizable theology of the Hebrew Scriptures? The place of readers in the interpretive process becomes important to the scholarly task, and I suggest that readers in our setting find it helpful to have a framework for reading. Readers who are aware of contexts and appropriate reading strategies for those contexts and who are critically aware of assumptions brought into the reading process produce more historically informed and theologically perceptive readings of texts. Crafting a satisfying shape for an Old

Testament theology gives readers beneficial frameworks and contexts for interpretation. Reading individual texts in light of the context of the whole is an important part of the interpretive process. Context is central to clarifying a text's distinctive contribution. Such frameworks will need to be both coherent and flexible. That is, they will need to account for both the diversity and the unity of the Older Testament. The Old Testament includes both the traditional wisdom of Proverbs and Job's challenges to that wisdom. Leviticus and Deuteronomy include differing legal perspectives. Within the pages of the Old Testament are both ancestral narratives and prophetic/poetic oracles. Both historical narrative and poetry are inherent to the nature of the Older Testament. Are there theological labels comprehensive enough and adaptable enough to organize the faith of the Hebrew Scriptures in ways that will meaningfully assist theological interpreters? Can these labels interact in productive ways? How might interpreters proceed?

Recent Works

A number of works from these first decades of the twenty-first century suggest that the theological study of the Hebrew Scriptures remains a part of the agenda of biblical scholarship. It will be helpful to review these in search of a path forward. Careful attention to our shared scholarly history, including recent history, can give helpful direction. Some of these works are included in the review earlier in the chapter but deserve more comment in this context.

Erhard Gerstenberger's volume reflects several of the recent trends in theological scholarship on the Older Testament. The title *Theologies in the Old Testament* suggests the emphasis on diversity in the theological structures of the Old Testament. His perspective relates to his lived experience and to the views of liberation theology. He categorizes the theological perspectives in the Old Testament by way of sociological categories. The diversity of theological views is the result of Israel's changing sociohistorical contexts. Each social setting generates a distinct theological perspective: family/clan, city, and nation, for example.

In insisting on the diversity and development of Israelite conceptions of God, Gerstenberger rejects the pursuit to find a "center" to their theology: "The Old Testament, a collection of many testimonies of faith from around a thousand years of the history of ancient Israel, has no unitary theology, nor can it."[37] In addition to his consideration of ancient Israel's context, Gerstenberger also insists that the context of theologians/scholars bears upon their conclusions. He argues that "any exegesis of the Old Testament and any 'theology' of the Old Testament based on it, is subject to its own limited, concrete, contextual conditions and therefore cannot be absolutized."[38] Interpreters cannot separate themselves fully from their own backgrounds and convictions, and therefore objective theology is simply not possible.

John Goldingay produced three volumes of Old Testament theology in the first decade of the twenty-first century.[39] His perspective reflects the concerns of a Christian theologian who is a longtime seminary teacher and somewhat evangelical in perspective. His methodology is best characterized as a narrative approach. He reviews the shape of texts in the First Testament—as he labels it—and attends to their theological perspectives. He narrates the story of the ancient Israelite community. Moving through the Old Testament literature in a narrative progression, Goldingay traces the work of salvation. This salvation history is first restricted to the people of Israel, but ultimately opened toward all people. God is revealed through very specific historical events portrayed within the Old Testament, beginning with creation. Throughout these robust volumes, Goldingay is careful to articulate the unity and diversity of the Hebrew canon and the relationship of this material to the Christian church.

The important volume by Terence Fretheim is in some ways a culmination of the rediscovery noted above of the centrality of creation theology in the Hebrew Scriptures.[40] Organizing his work around the

---

37. Gerstenberger, *Theologies in the Old Testament*, 1.
38. Gerstenberger, *Theologies in the Old Testament*, 13.
39. Goldingay, *Old Testament Theology*.
40. Fretheim, *God and World in the Old Testament*.

view that Israel primarily understood God first and foremost as creator, Fretheim emphasizes texts that articulate creation perspectives
in the Older Testament. He naturally spends considerable time on
texts in Genesis. The fact that the Old Testament itself begins with
creation and not the exodus is foundational for Fretheim. Even within
texts in which previous theologians used to highlight God's role as
redeemer, such as Exodus 15, Fretheim highlights the prevalence of
creation language. Many texts demonstrate that Israel understood
God who redeemed them from Egypt as the *creator* God. Creation
includes not just the beginning of the cosmos but also God's ongoing work. The Old Testament itself understands creation in this
broader sense—creation does entail the original work of creation,
but more often (especially in the prophets) God's work is spoken of
as continuing creative activity in and through historical processes.
Fretheim names three interrelated points of reference for creation:
originating creation, continuing creation, and completing creation.
For him, God has promised to uphold the future of creation, but God
is not a micromanager who controls every detail. Creation is reliable
and trustworthy, but not a predetermined, fixed system. Completed
creation refers to God's eschatological work in bringing about a new
heaven and earth. Fretheim calls for a relational model of creation that
focuses on the interrelatedness of God and creatures. All creatures are
dependent on God for life and sustenance, but God has actually chosen to establish an interdependent relationship with the created order
and share the responsibility of sustaining creation. Creatures—human
and nonhuman—are given a part in creative activity for God's own
sake. Fretheim names a *mutuality of vocation* between humans and
nonhumans, in service of each other and God. While humans seem
to have been given a special responsibility at creation, the nonhuman
creation has a vocation as well.

Rolf Rendtorff's work on Old Testament theology has for a number
of years emphasized the importance of the canon. His work follows
the trajectory of Childs's perspective though in a different context, a
more recent and European one. Rendtorff is particularly concerned

with Jewish-Christian relationships and how they relate to the Old Testament or Hebrew Scriptures. Specifically, Rendtorff insists that we read the Hebrew Bible in and of itself as a theological text without reference to the New Testament.[41] Rendtorff's *The Canonical Hebrew Bible* is organized into two main sections with a final third part containing two brief essays regarding the methodological assumptions of a "canonical" approach and the problems inherent in a theological reading of a corpus shared by two communities of faith. Part 1 contains a synchronic theological commentary on the entire Hebrew Bible, following the Torah-Nevi'im-Ketuvim ordering of the Jewish Scriptures. Rendtorff begins his task, fittingly, with Genesis 1:1 and the primeval history. He discusses the theological centrality of the power of God's word and highlights God's creative activities and the link between God's creation and the world of humans. Rendtorff follows the narrative actions of two central characters: YHWH and Moses. In the Former Prophets, Rendtorff outlines the pattern of initial blessing and eventual decline that characterizes not only the reigns of David and Solomon but the entire period of the monarchy. Rendtorff next moves to the Ketuvim, or Writings. Theological interpretation begins within the Bible itself, and in many ways, the Writings and the Prophets are themselves theological reflections on the Torah. This perspective is especially important for the Psalter, which highlights the importance of living a Torah-centered life by framing the entire collection with Torah-concerned psalms (Pss. 1–2, 150).

In the second section, Rendtorff adopts a thematic structure similar to that of Childs. He deals with topics as they arise in canonical order and proceeds with exposition along lexical and conceptual lines. Rendtorff's goal with this approach is to account for the majority of biblical occurrences of any given theme without attempting to harmonize or systematize his findings beyond the text. Rendtorff's synchronic reading serves, in his mind, as the last stage in a diachronic

41. Rendtorff, *Canonical Hebrew Bible*.

reading of the text—that is, How would its contents be understood at the moment of final compilation? He argues that undue scholarly focus has been placed on earlier iterations of the text to the detriment of the theological and literary genius of the tradents responsible for the final form of the texts.

John Rogerson's major contribution to Old Testament theology came in 2010.[42] He seeks to communicate the beliefs of the ancient Israelites in a way that directly addresses today's world. Rogerson's key term throughout the book is "communicative." "The agenda will be set subjectively, not by means drawn directly from the Old Testament, but from the author's intellectual predilections and his reflections on the plight of humanity living in today's world(s)."[43] His intention is to utilize the tools of modern critical scholarship to interrogate the Old Testament texts because they have something to say to the present. Rogerson uses what he calls a "narrative view" of history, meaning that all we have to construct the past are narratives that have been created by human beings who have limited knowledge and presuppositions. What is most important about the biblical text is that it is a witness to the belief in God. Because of this, Rogerson approaches the text not in a historical fashion but through the use of "cultural memory." Rogerson then, via Lévi-Strauss, identifies and explains two types of history writing, "hot" and "cold." Hot histories (e.g., the Deuteronomistic history) internalize the historical processes as they are questioning, open to change, and hold out hope. Cold histories (e.g., Chronicles) are constructed to show continuity with the past and foster a sense of legitimacy through historical connection. In chapter 2 Rogerson explicates hot and cold retellings of the creation account. He identifies what he calls "founding memories" as Genesis 1, 8–9; Job 38–41; Ecclesiastes 1; Jonah; and a few psalms. He argues that all of these are "hot" accounts because they seek to challenge the status quo of the present by portraying the past as ideal and encouraging change in the present. A cold account preserves the status quo

---

42. Rogerson, *Theology of the Old Testament*.
43. Rogerson, *Theology of the Old Testament*, 11.

in social relations. The latter part of the volume focuses on what it means to be human. Here Rogerson develops the notion that growth in humane qualities and actions brings growth toward life in the image of God.

Three volumes appeared in 2013. John Kessler's approach operates from the categories of divine call and human response.[44] He calls this work "an introduction to the OT's theological world." The theological streams that he considers are creation theology, covenant theology, promise theology, priestly theology, the theology of divine accessibility (namely, the Psalms and other prayers), and wisdom theology. All of these streams offer ways of thinking about the relationship between God and Israel or, in other words, about God's call and the human response to that call.

Mark McEntire's volume follows a narrative approach to the characterization of God as a means to pursuing the theological perspective of the Older Testament.[45] Specifically, he highlights the diversity of portrayals of God within the Old Testament. McEntire offers a narrative theology covering the entire Hebrew Bible, demonstrating the contrast between the "mighty acts of God" in its earlier parts and the more subtle and behind-the-scenes ways in which God acts in such books as Ezra-Nehemiah. McEntire observes that many previous Old Testament theology works focus on the dramatic activity of God in the earlier books of the Hebrew Bible but neglect the later books. He argues that the end point of the story is more important, and so he seeks to offer the "mature God," "the God at the end of the story."

Walter Moberly's work explores theological dimensions of the Old Testament.[46] This book does not attempt a comprehensive theology of the Old Testament in the manner of von Rad, Eichrodt, or Brueggemann. Rather, Moberly's volume is a collection of essays revised and edited into a coherent work that is selective and discursive. Each chapter considers major topics in Old Testament theology within

---

44. Kessler, *Old Testament Theology.*
45. McEntire, *Portraits of a Mature God.*
46. Moberly, *Old Testament Theology.*

a particularly Christian reading yet still in dialogue with Jewish interpreters.

Konrad Schmid has recently brought a most interesting perspective to this area of study.[47] He is keenly aware of the academic context in Germany, and to the question of whether there is theology in the Hebrew Bible he answers in the negative. His definition of "theology" is very specific, an academic—one might say scholastic—definition of traditional theology. Theology would be a systematic articulation of doctrines from a specific church tradition. That perspective is not the perspective of the Hebrew Bible. It is telling that Schmid uses that academic title ("Hebrew Bible") for the collection. The Hebrew Scriptures clearly communicate theological content, but the definition of "theology" needs to be much broader to fit the current context of theological discourse. Chapter 3 is the heart of the volume, as Schmid explicates a significant distinction between implicit and explicit theology. He finds that the most important texts of implicit theology are found in works of expansion literature, works that emerged during the Babylonian, Persian, and Hellenistic periods, developing the early content of Israel's traditions.

Most of the Old Testament theology works in the twenty-first century seek to navigate in one way or another the shattered spectrum discussed above. Schmid's work is distinct in that it clearly depends on historical-critical work on the Hebrew Bible. In doing so, his work is liable to the critiques of earlier works tied to a construction of history that will change with the generations of scholars. His recent volume reflects current European historical-critical scholarship.[48] The volume is a sophisticated and impressive review of issues and themes in the theological study of the Hebrew Bible. It does not attend to questions of structuring a theology of the Older Testament. He indicates that the Hebrew Bible preserved in literary form a significant reception history rather than a religion lived in a historical community.

47. K. Schmid, *Is There Theology in the Hebrew Bible?*
48. K. Schmid, *Historical Theology of the Hebrew Bible.*

Table 1. Key Old Testament Theologies

Author	Title	Date	Approach
The Era of Eichrodt and von Rad			
W. Eichrodt	*Theology of the Old Testament (2 vols.)*	1933–39	Synchronic; center: covenant
L. Köhler	*Old Testament Theology*	1936	Center: lordship of God
T. Vriezen	*An Outline of Old Testament Theology*	1949	Center: communion
G. von Rad	*Old Testament Theology (2 vols.)*	1957–60	Diachronic
The Latter Part of the Twentieth Century			
C. Westermann	*Elements of Old Testament Theology*	1978	History/creation themes
S. Terrien	*The Elusive Presence*	1978	History/creation themes
B. Childs	*Old Testament Theology in a Canonical Context*	1989	Canonical
L. Perdue	*The Collapse of History*	1994	History of scholarship
W. Brueggemann	*Theology of the Old Testament*	1997	Metaphorical
Recent Works			
K. Schmid	*A Historical Theology of the Hebrew Bible*	2018	Historical-critical

Conclusion

This account of the story of Old Testament theology has raised many questions. The narrative of this modern area of academic study begins with the assertion of the independence of the discipline. The Hebrew (or Aramaic) text is the primary literature, and scholars are here asking what it affirms about God. The New Testament and the church or synagogue are related to the task of this discipline but do not determine it. The assumptions of the interpreter are also relevant and significant in how one relates the Older Testament to communities of faith and to narratives of faith. The key is to stay as close as is humanly possible to the perspective the Hebrew text articulates about God and divine-human engagement. Old Testament theologians have most often argued for some kind of coherence in narrating the theological perspectives of this text. That coherence takes a variety of forms and is currently under considerable strain. Many postmodern and many Jewish interpreters are not terribly interested in such coherence; it is not central to their traditions.[49] Indeed, a number of postmodern interpreters are tentative about affirming the divine in our post-Holocaust, chaotic, and frighteningly violent context. These realities threaten the future of Old Testament theology and must be taken seriously in this academic arena. The context in which scholars operate is a crucial part of the picture.

The quote from Walter Brueggemann noted early in this chapter still holds true: the comprehensive designs of Eichrodt and von Rad are important and past. Eichrodt's synchronic approach and emphasis on covenant as the center (*die Mitte*) produced many insights. Von Rad's emphasis on the various theological traditions and on salvation history in a diachronic approach also contributes in vital ways. The historical-critical study of the Old Testament continues to contribute immeasurably to the discipline. In addition, Childs's emphasis on the canon or Hebrew text as guide is crucial to the task, but this chapter raised a number of questions about the ways Childs pursued the task. Perdue's image of the "shattered spectrum" rules the day. We now need to find new paths in this discipline. Brueggemann has sought a way forward with the courtroom as the metaphorical context in which the Old Testament's testimony comes to light. His account is a robust one, but this chapter has raised questions about both the metaphor and his account of ancient Israel's testimony. So we still look for new ways

49. See Levenson, "Why Jews Are Not Interested in Biblical Theology." Levenson cites as one early reason for the distance Jewish biblicists have kept from biblical theology the "intense anti-Semitism which is evident in many of the classic works in that field," as well as deprecatory remarks about Rabbinic Judaism (287). Levenson also points out, however, that many Jews were driven to a more historical reconstruction not because of faith but because of the lack of it: "They approached the past—even the biblical past—in hopes not of defining a theology but of finding a replacement for theology" (318). In general, however, Jewish interpretation is not concerned with identifying one overarching idea or theme that pervades and unifies the Hebrew Bible. Jewish thought is much more comfortable with the polydoxy of biblical theology than is Christianity (320, 322). Scripture is multifaceted, and each facet deserves attention.

forward. I suggest that we are in search of a way to begin and a way to proceed. The history of the discipline recounted in this chapter will inform that search considerably. The discipline's shattered spectrum and the interpreters' chaotic contexts bring considerable challenges. Theological diversity and pluralism shape our day. What kind of way forward might be possible?

Our look at the narrative of the subject area of Old Testament theology has left us with many questions. Eichrodt and von Rad developed two classic approaches, and Childs's work articulated significant issues that led him to emphasize canon as the context for pursuing Old Testament theology. Brueggemann's metaphorical approach provides a robust attempt to come to terms with the extensive theological perspectives of the Older Testament. Still, the plurality of theological witnesses in the text and the "shattered spectrum" of interpretations leave many challenges for today's students and scholars alike. Theological purposes also come into play for theologians committed to communities of faith. "The search for coherent Old Testament theological structures is a significant part of biblical theology."[50] Such frameworks assist in the daunting tasks of embracing these ancient texts that are increasingly unfamiliar to contemporary readers. The number of recent works on theological perspectives in the Older Testament suggests that in the first decades of the twenty-first century, those who study the Hebrew Bible are actively questioning starting places, methodologies, and organizations. That is an encouraging trend. So how might we begin to pursue these questions?

My proposal is shaped by the narrative introduced in the introduction and the first chapter. We learn much from the paths scholars have taken up to this point, but we are called on to find new paths. There is no one "center" to define the study of Old Testament theology. The pluralism of our day is a central reality in our work as Old Testament theologians; questions abound when we base our work on traditional historical-critical efforts. Questions of where we begin and how we

50. Bellinger, "Psalms as a Place to Begin for Old Testament Theology," 30.

proceed from that beginning are pivotal. I propose a textual starting point, one in which the ancient community confessed its faith. And I will suggest that this textual starting point reveals three theological perspectives that constitute faith confessed as contributing to wholeness in the divine-human engagement, to the gift of believing and living fully. Along the way, we will see that this proposal makes a larger place for the Wisdom literature than have a number of the proposals discussed in this chapter. The literary dimensions of the proposal seek to embrace the whole of the Hebrew canon and deal with questions central to faith for the ancient worshiping community and the contemporary one. The divine gift of life, the response of creation and its creatures, and all the implications of that engagement reverberate through the canon. This perspective calls readers to fully explore this engagement not as a historical artifact but as a contemporary hope.

2

A Shape for Old Testament Theology

A Starting Point

So now we seek a path ahead. If those of us who read the Older Testament are to pursue these questions, Bernhard Anderson suggests, "we must find a valid starting point in the midst of the multiplex literature of the Old Testament."[1] Where should interpreters look? If the task is to find the faith confessed in the Old Testament, perhaps the fullest source for the ancient community's articulation of faith is the Psalms. An important articulation of this perspective is the presidential address for the Society of Old Testament Study published in 1963 by George W. Anderson, "Israel's Creed: Sung, Not Signed." G. Anderson understands the Old Testament to be at base a confessional document from a worshiping community. He suggests that in the psalms the community sang its faith and that Psalms constitutes a theological synthesis of this faith. He supports this view with three perspectives from the Psalms.

1. B. Anderson, *Contours of Old Testament Theology*, 19.

First, the range of Old Testament literature is present in the Psalter. Included are the recitation of history and the community's experience with monarchy. There is also the celebration of Torah and of wisdom, as well as the voice of prophecy in terms of both judgment and instruction. Second, Psalms bears witness to problems inherent to the task of shaping an Old Testament theology. A diversity of theological perspectives is present in the Psalms. The question of how one relates the Psalms to the history of ancient Israel's religion and the various contexts found in it also comes to the fore in the interpretation of the Psalms. G. Anderson opines, "The Psalter represents a remarkable concentration of these and other problems of theological interpretation and thus exemplifies uniquely the recalcitrance of the Old Testament material to our attempt to reduce it to a propositional confessional system which adherents might be required to sign."[2] Third, the Psalter includes the theological themes characteristic of the Older Testament: "Election and covenant, rejection and restoration, *Heilsgeschichte*, creation and providence, the way of life and the way of death."[3]

The Psalter as a diverse collection of psalms coheres as a confession of a worshiping community, in terms of prayer and praise from this community as it encounters YHWH and confesses faith in YHWH as the community's God. Psalms concentrates and selects theological material unlike any other part of the Hebrew Scriptures and is shaped in the context of ancient Israel's worship. Its contents both came from the life of the community and shaped the life of the community. The Psalter shows how this ancient faith community sang its creed and so confessed its God. Thus, G. Anderson suggests that the Psalter provides guidance for those engaged in the tasks characterizing Old Testament theology.

I am essentially in agreement with G. Anderson's view. Psalms is representative of the theology of the Older Testament, and in the Psalms the ancient worshiping community sings its faith. The Psalter is at the center of the Old Testament and its theological viewpoint. If we

2. G. Anderson, "Israel's Creed," 283.
3. G. Anderson, "Israel's Creed," 284.

somehow lost the rest of the Old Testament but retained the Psalter, we would still have the basics to construct an Old Testament theology. So, to use B. Anderson's language, I suggest that the "starting point" for our task is not a center in the sense of the German *die Mitte*, the kind of center Eichrodt argued for when he said covenant is the center from which Old Testament theology is structured. I suggest rather a textual starting point, the Psalms, as our guide. Two implications of this approach are noteworthy. First, it suggests that the most fruitful context for shaping a theology is a worshiping community. Second, the Psalter most frequently articulates the initiative for God's engagement with the world as coming from the divine side. This chapter will pursue both of these points.

A more recent articulation of G. Anderson's view comes from William Brown:

> If not the theological center of the Old Testament, the Psalter is at least Scripture's most integrated corpus. On David's many-stringed lyre, as it were, there can be heard almost every theological chord that resounds throughout the Hebrew Scriptures, from covenant and history to creation and wisdom. In the Psalms, the God who commands is also the God who sustains. The God of royal pedigree and the God of the "poor and needy," the God of judgment and the God of healing, God's hidden face and God's beaming countenance: all are profiled in the Psalter. It was not without justification that Luther called the Psalter "the little Bible."[4]

My most recent volume on the Psalms argues for understanding the prayer and praise of the Psalter as a grammar of faith centering on worship and on the dialogue with YHWH.[5] My reading of the Psalter is in line with both Anderson's and Brown's. The Psalter is at the center of Old Testament faith and thus provides a very promising starting place for the work of Old Testament theologians.

4. Brown, *Seeing the Psalms*, 1.
5. Bellinger, *Psalms as a Grammar for Faith*.

Divine-Human Engagement

When we begin with the Psalter, what do we discover about God in relation to humanity? I suggest that there are three verbs that imply key theological themes.[6]

First, God *delivers*. Psalm 107 begins the fifth book of Psalms with a series of vignettes that illustrate the trouble and woe God's people encounter followed by divine deliverance. Verse 6 straightforwardly articulates this deliverance.

> Then they cried to the LORD in their trouble,
>   and he delivered them from their distress.

The latter part of the psalm reflects more broadly on this theme. Other psalms of thanksgiving narrate or declare for the congregation God's deliverance from trouble. Psalms of descriptive praise recount in classic hymnic form the memory of God's deliverance of the community. Lament psalms constitute the most frequent genre in the Psalms; these gripping poems plead with God to enact the promise of deliverance from the trouble and woe at hand.

Other parts of the Older Testament also bear witness to this confession that God delivers. The paradigmatic narrative from this perspective is the story of the exodus from Egypt. Exodus 3 articulates the paradigm.

> Then the LORD said, "I have observed the misery of my people who are in Egypt; I have heard their cry on account of their taskmasters. Indeed, I know their sufferings, and I have come down to deliver them from the Egyptians, and to bring them up out of that land to a good and broad land, a land flowing with milk and honey, to the country of the Canaanites, the Hittites, the Amorites, the Perizzites, the Hivites, and the Jebusites. The cry of the Israelites has now come to me; I have also seen how the Egyptians oppress them." (vv. 7–9)

6. See Bellinger, "Portraits of Faith," 111–28.

The Hebrew Scriptures recount a history of God's deliverance: from Egypt, through the wilderness, and then in conflicts with Canaanite peoples as well as the dominating Mesopotamian empires. It is characteristic of these texts that divine intervention to deliver issues in the formation of a covenant relationship between YHWH and the people. Thus, the verb "delivers" implies the perspective of covenant theology. My proposed shape for Old Testament theology also recognizes that divine revelation calls for a human response. When the divine revelation takes the form of covenant, the avenue of human response is divine instruction or *torah*. Much of the Pentateuch, especially the book of Exodus, and much of the historical books of the Old Testament emphasize this theological tradition. It is clear from the paradigmatic story and from these additional texts that at the fore of this theological angle of vision comes the human cry for help in the middle of trouble and woe. This urgent cry initiates the divine embrace of pain and deliverance. *In summary, the first theological stream is covenant theology in which God delivers, and the avenue of human response is* torah.

Second, God *blesses*. An important distinction bubbles to the surface in this confession of faith. In the first theological perspective, God comes to deliver in historical events that texts recount in the Hebrew Bible. In this second theological perspective, God is present to bless. Blessing is an ongoing life experience. "Blessing is about the gift of wholeness or shalom in life rather than about God's revelation in history through the act of delivering the people."[7] The works of Claus Westermann reflect this distinction.[8] The Psalms confess God as creator and ruler, the one present in Zion to bless, the one who is worthy of trust. Blessing can be defined as the power to grow and thrive in the world, made possible by the divine presence. Psalm 134:3, in the climax of the Songs of Ascent, offers blessing.

> May the LORD, maker of heaven and earth,
> bless you from Zion.

7. Bellinger, "Shape for Old Testament Theology," 294.
8. Cf. Westermann, *What Does the Old Testament Say about God?*; Westermann, *Elements of Old Testament Theology*; and Westermann, *Blessing in the Bible and in the Life of the Church*.

The Songs of Ascent sing of the divine presence with the community and of the divine guidance of the community. Blessing is central to the hymns of praise in the Psalter. The royal psalms and the wisdom psalms also affirm divine blessing by way of the Davidic king and by way of the gift of wisdom, respectively.

The broader Old Testament confession of faith in the divine blessing begins in Genesis 1. God creates the world and humans and provides for full living.

> God blessed them, and God said to them, "Be fruitful and multiply, and fill the earth and subdue it; and have dominion over the fish of the sea and over the birds of the air and over every living thing that moves upon the earth." (v. 28)

The divine blessing is also crucial to the familiar call of Abram in Genesis 12.

> Now the LORD said to Abram, "Go from your country and your kindred and your father's house to the land that I will show you. I will make of you a great nation, and I will bless you, and make your name great, so that you will be a blessing. I will bless those who bless you, and the one who curses you I will curse; and in you all the families of the earth shall be blessed." (vv. 1–3)

This text makes it clear that the divine blessing is not so much a privilege as it is a reality to be shared with others. These ancestors were called to be good stewards of this blessing. God makes it possible for the blessing to survive and thrive through the generations of the ancestors. Then there is also the blessing of the land and life therein and the mixed blessing of the kingdoms and their monarchies. With all these in mind, the verb "bless" implies the perspective of creation theology.

Whereas the means of human response to God's delivering through covenant was *torah*, the means of human response to God's blessing through creation is found in wisdom. Wisdom is necessary in caring for and sharing the divine blessing. Wisdom is given by the creator and learned by the community. Genesis, additional Priestly texts, and royal texts all operate from this perspective. In this theological perspective, wisdom as a means of human response makes considerable space for questions about suffering and the mysteries of life. *So, the second stream is creation theology in which God is present to bless, and the path of human response is found in wisdom.*

Third, God *speaks*. The Psalms characterize God as one who instructs on worship and one who warns. Two formative psalms in the first book of the Psalter—Psalms 15 and 24—are categorized as entrance liturgies or entrance *toroth*. They portray those who are prepared for worship in the sanctuary.

> Who shall ascend the hill of the LORD?
>   And who shall stand in his holy place?
> Those who have clean hands and pure hearts,
>   who do not lift up their souls to what is false,
>   and do not swear deceitfully. (24:3–4)

The qualifications for worship (v. 4) come in the voice of the priest as the representative of God. The qualifications tend to be more ethical than ritual. Several of the hymns of praise include prophetic warnings in direct divine speech.

> Hear, O my people, and I will speak,
>   O Israel, I will testify against you.
> I am God, your God. (50:7)

An important part of this emphasis in the Psalms is actively listening to the divine voice.

> But my people did not listen to my voice;
>   Israel would not submit to me.
> So I gave them over to their stubborn hearts,
>   to follow their own counsels.

> O that my people would listen to me,
>   that Israel would walk in my ways! (81:11–13)

This theological perspective we rightly list third in an attempt to characterize divine engagement portrayed in the Psalter. Contemporary scholars would likely attach the label of theological ethics to such texts, which are unmistakably an essential part of this worshiping community's confession of faith. In the broader Old Testament, this picture of divine engagement with the world is primarily focused on the prophetic tradition of faith in the Hebrew Scriptures found in the Latter Prophets and their proclamations of divine judgment and mercy. Amos rails against social injustice, and Hosea grieves over idolatry in the community. Isaiah 40–55 majestically speaks of faith centered on God's bringing about something new, a second exodus, now an exodus from the north, an exodus out of exile. These texts are but a few examples of the extensive prophetic corpus in which God speaks. In a sense, the Prophets intertwine the recitations of God's delivering and God's blessing while at the same time making a new beginning centering on the spoken divine word. Thus, the verb "speaks" implies the perspective of prophetic theology.

God's speech consistently calls for a faithful response from the worshiping community. The prophetic word calls the hearing community to repent—that is, to orient one's life in new and different ways, in ways attuned to faith, justice, hope, and righteousness. The primary texts involved here are the Latter Prophets: Isaiah, Jeremiah, Ezekiel, and the Twelve (Hosea, Joel, Amos, Obadiah, Jonah, Micah, Nahum, Habakkuk, Zephaniah, Haggai, Zechariah, and Malachi). This poetic/prophetic corpus also makes a new literary beginning, constituting its own unit in the Hebrew Bible. Essential in this prophetic tradition are the divine pathos seen in God's continuing to stay with the community fully even in the midst of their crises and troubles and the human pathos where the community works to form a common life in the shared experiences of joy and suffering. *The third stream is prophetic theology, in which God speaks and looks for a response of repentance.*

Implications

So far in this chapter, I have begun by suggesting that we take the liturgical book of Psalms as a starting point for the shape of Old Testament theology, and I have suggested three perspectives to that starting point: (1) covenant theology, in which God comes to deliver and the means of response is *torah* or divine instruction; (2) creation theology, in which God is present to bless and the path of human response is wisdom; and (3) prophetic theology in which this God speaks and the manner of human response is repentance. Together, these perspectives form the three-legged stool on which the message of the Hebrew Scriptures rests. I have not attempted to encompass every piece of the Hebrew canon in this shape for an Old Testament theology. Rather, I am seeking to construct a framework or context for critically informed readers. Conceiving of God as creator, deliverer, and speaker prepares the reader for a divine-human encounter which in turn brings wholeness, a life of prayer, joy, and healthy community—that is, salvation.

Rather than present the message of the Hebrew Scriptures under these three topics of covenant, creation, and prophecy, I find it more interesting and more beneficial to work through the various sections of the canon—Pentateuch, Former Prophets, Psalms, Wisdom (the two combine to make up the Writings), and Latter Prophets—with these three perspectives in mind to see how they interact in order to shape constructive theological formation. That is, in part, an influence of Childs.

This proposal of a shape for an Old Testament theology seeks to take into account the lessons of the history of research recounted in the first chapter. I have sought to account for the theological diversity of the Older Testament in the tradition of Brueggemann while at the same time structuring an organizational plan as Eichrodt would suggest. I am also attentive to issues related to history, as was von Rad. This shape for a theology of the Hebrew Scriptures begins with the text and gives some attention to readers. That procedure is in line with the hermeneutical view that meaning is constructed in the interaction between texts and readers. In this constructive work, I do not seek to avoid history and do not think that route is credible in any case. The Hebrew Bible comes to us in the guise of classical Hebrew language and so reflects the originating culture or social setting of that language. As with any text, the intentions of its producers (authors) and their cultural codes are imbedded in the text. Interpreters need to attend to those historical realities. At the same time, interpreters need to recognize our lack of direct access to such histories. We need to interact with all we can learn about such matters of composition and sociohistorical contexts, but the shape I have proposed is not directly based on those historical conclusions about specific cultural contexts. My sense is that there is continuity between history and the text of the Hebrew Scriptures, "but that relationship is fraught with questions."[9] Crucial for any informed reading of the Old Testament is careful attendance to the gift of the scholarly work of those who have come before us. That is but one essential part in the important task of working in conversation with others, especially given our postmodern context.

In some ways, this approach to organizing an Old Testament theology owes a debt to those in the late 1970s who followed what was called a bipolar organization. As noted in the previous chapter, Westermann, Terrien, and Hanson, among others, suggested that one center for organizing an Old Testament theology was insufficient in the face of the theological diversity in the canon, but two major theological perspectives in constructive dialogue with each other could better accommodate such diversity. In some ways, covenant and creation as theological perspectives are similar to the themes these scholars propose. The themes mutually support, complement, and raise cautions about each other. Neither of the themes is secondary, contrary to both H. H. Schmid's understanding of covenant as renewing the dominant theme of creation and von Rad's representation of creation as secondary to salvation history (or covenant). By "theological perspectives" I am suggesting that the two perspectives reflect distinctive patterns for portraying divine engagement with the human community.

9. Bellinger, "Shape for Old Testament Theology," 295.

A Tripartite Shape

Covenant theology characterizes divine engagement with the world in terms of deliverance from a crisis. It is a deliverance beyond the capabilities of the human community. God delivered the ancient Hebrew community from oppression in Egypt. This liberation is of divine initiative and is in the form of an event. So, YHWH comes to deliver the people from Egyptian bondage, and the text recounts this deliverance and reveals to the people that YHWH will be their God and the people will be YHWH's people. The outcome of the liberation from Egypt is a covenant relationship between YHWH and the community Moses leads. The image is of God's reaching down to pull the people up from a deep, distressing hole out of which they could not climb. That event initiates a covenant relationship, complete with divine instructions for life in this new community—in the Decalogue and covenant code, for example. The liturgical community remembers and celebrates such events of deliverance and such life-giving instruction. Whether the people respond in obedience is highly consequential. Large blocks of Old Testament text operate out of this image of divine-human engagement.

Creation theology understands divine engagement with the world in terms of blessing for living. Blessing is the power to grow and thrive in the world, and it is made possible by the divine presence. So, blessing relates to an ongoing condition or experience in life. It comes from an undergirding divine presence that authorizes wholeness in life for the community. From Zion YHWH authorizes hope, power, and growth for persons and for the community. It is a benediction that comes from the experience of the divine in worship and continues to make wholeness possible in life. When God created humans, God blessed them, identifying them as those created in the divine image, as those who represent God in maintaining and enjoying and sharing what is provided for full life together in community. This blessed life is fed in worship and the divine presence to bless therein. This blessing comes from the creator and is encountered in creation in a continuing way. Responsible living as those in God's image in creation is learned as wisdom. When God created the world, God placed wisdom in it and enabled people to find that wisdom. People of faith learn wisdom from teachers or sages, who pass on this wisdom to students. Proverbs, Job, and Ecclesiastes likewise bequeath such wisdom and call the community to learn it.

These first elements of the shape being proposed for an Old Testament theology are dependent in some ways on the views of Westermann.[10] Covenant and creation theology are not neatly separated or independent in the Older Testament. It is not that Genesis operates from creation theology and Exodus operates from covenant theology. Strands of both theological perspectives run through both books. While Genesis emphasizes the blessing God in creation—who is present to provide for and authorize full living for humanity and for the ancestral generations—it also includes covenant perspectives—for example, in the Noahic covenant with all of creation and the ancestral covenant promise. The confirmation of the promise with a covenant ceremony in Genesis 15 and the covenant of circumcision in Genesis 17 reflect that perspective, and the tradition of theophanies in the ancestral stories portrays a God who comes in the form of messengers to deliver on occasion. In Exodus the dominant perspective in the first half of the book is that of covenant theology. The Moses story is about the oppression of ancient Israel in Egypt; God as the covenant-making God hears their lament and comes to deliver them from this crisis. The background and call of Moses and the narrative of the plagues in Egypt reveal this God who comes to deliver. This same God then appears to the community at Sinai and provides them with instruction in covenant living in the Decalogue and the Covenant Code. The covenant is agreed to between YHWH and Israel. The consequences of the community's response to the covenant instruction become clear as the narrative continues. The golden calf narrative in Exodus 32–34 illustrates the breaking and the renewing of the covenant relationship between YHWH and Israel. Yet the latter part of Exodus (chapters 25–40) moves back to a creation

---

10. See especially Westermann, *What Does the Old Testament Say about God?*

perspective, with instructions for the construction of the tabernacle as a place of worship and provision of leadership for worship. The tabernacle is constructed, and the book concludes with affirmation of the mobile sanctuary as a place of divine presence, a manifestation of the creator's blessing (Exod. 40:34–38).

Joining the perspectives of both creation and covenant theologies helps to present a full portrayal of divine involvement with the world and with humanity. Covenant theology by itself, with the mighty acts of God in coming to deliver, produces a God of the gaps who is involved in history only in events. The creator who blesses is present in a continuing way and so is able to make possible growth and wholeness in everyday living and in the high points of festival life. The perspectives are complementary. The two theological perspectives together give a fuller portrait of YHWH and YHWH's engagement with the world and its human community.

Perceptive readers will realize that so far, I have focused on the Torah, the Former Prophets, and the Writings. What about the Latter Prophets? What merits regarding these as a third leg? First, this part of the Hebrew canon makes a new literary beginning. It is true that prophetic characters appear in the Former Prophets, and the Latter Prophets' view of ancient Israel's history and experience also infuses those narratives. But while the Former Prophets primarily consist of narratives, the Latter Prophets are primarily poetic proclamations. In the prophetic tradition of the Second Temple period, prophecy moved more toward a prose style. The phenomenon of prophecy was characteristic of the ancient Near East and was woven into ancient Israel's life. Its classical style can be labeled as poetic preaching of righteousness. It speaks to the consequences of the spiritual life of the community. Abraham Joshua Heschel defines prophecy as the exegesis of the present from God's point of view.[11] Prophets are pictured as mediators of a divine message. This phenomenon of delivering a divine message eventually entered ancient Israel's practice of the scribal preservation of texts, and

11. Heschel, *Prophets*, 1:29–31.

so prophecy moved into written form and was studied and preserved and edited on the way to becoming a crucial dimension of the Hebrew Bible. So the literary distinctiveness of the Latter Prophets is the first rationale for labeling them as the third leg of this tripartite shape for Old Testament theology.

Second, the Latter Prophets portray divine engagement with the world in a distinctive way: God speaks. The prophets are characterized as carrying the messages God speaks from the divine throne room to the community. They are responsible for understanding these revelatory experiences and messages and crafting a way to deliver them to the community of faith. The phrase *koh 'amar YHWH*, "thus says the LORD," is called the messenger formula, found also in international diplomacy when a diplomatic messenger delivers a message from one ruler to another. The prophet delivers a message from the divine ruler to the people of Israel. Heschel portrays the prophet as a messenger who screams the divine word or message into a loudspeaker.[12] So it is fair to describe the content of prophecy as divine speech. That is the way classical prophecy characterizes it—the word of the Lord. The prophet in speech and text reveals the divine message. This revelation takes a variety of literary forms. The prophet is central to determining the form of the communication. God's speaking calls the community to hear the message and repent (*shuv*). The Hebrew term has to do with stopping on a path of life and making a decision to turn around and move in a different direction, one characterized by faith, justice, wholeness, and right relationships with God and neighbor. So this third theological perspective centers on God's speaking and the call for the community to respond with repentance. It is a perspective both literarily and theologically distinct from creation and covenant theologies.

Third, the Latter Prophets imbed creation and covenant theologies into one another such that it is extraordinarily difficult to separate them. Both perspectives are present and intertwined; they are present

12. Heschel, *Prophets*, 1:xxii, 19.

in a different literary context, as noted above, and with the controlling dimension of revealing the God who speaks with a prophetic voice.

I offer three brief examples at this point. While interpretations of Amos vary, I think most interpreters would suggest that the book leans toward covenant. The social injustice pervading the community is a rejection of the covenant revelation of YHWH and of the covenant hopes for the community. At the same time, the first two chapters of the book focus on oracles against the nations, indicating that wisdom for living in YHWH's creation is available to those beyond Israel.[13] The book is also concerned with genuine worship and includes a series of doxologies (Amos 4:13; 5:8–9; 9:5–6) that utilize creation imagery. Both creation and covenant theology combine in Amos.

Hosea also derives from prophecies in the eighth century BCE in the Northern Kingdom of Israel. The primary issue in this prophetic word is idolatry. Israel's going after idols and indulging in the lifestyle and promises of fertility religions is analogous to adultery against YHWH. Chapter 4 of Hosea begins with a divine "indictment" against the people for their rejection of "faithfulness" and "loyalty" that has resulted in there being "no knowledge of God in the land." They have violated the covenant commandments of the Decalogue, as verse 2 indicates. The book calls for the people to return to the Lord (Hosea 6:1; 14:1). And yet, in Hosea 4:3 it is the creation that suffers from this covenant breaking. People, wild animals, birds, and fish suffer as the land mourns. Despite the centrality of genuine worship—a covenant theme—the book's concluding verse calls for wise understanding of Hosea's prophecy—a creation theme. Creation and covenant perspectives are deeply interconnected in this book.

A third example is the exilic voice of the prophet in the tradition of Isaiah (Isa. 40–55). These chapters center on a divine deliverance of the people, this time from exile in Babylon. Indeed, the powerful poetic prophecies speak of this divine deliverance as "a new thing" and as a second exodus. In this same prophetic word, hopeful prophecies make

---

13. Hans Walter Wolff (*Amos the Prophet*) understands Amos as a wisdom teacher. See also Clements, *Prophecy and Covenant*.

use of images centered on the renewal of creation and the watering of wilderness. The divine presence will deliver this dispirited community into a new creation. The primary concern is community disbelief in the God who is present to bless and comes to deliver. The prophetic word calls the community to repent of this disbelief and hope in God. This section of Isaiah artfully interweaves creation and covenant perspectives as the means of YHWH's speaking to the people and calling them to faithful living in light of this hopeful proclamation. It is difficult to cleanly separate the creation and covenant perspectives in these prophetic texts.

In sum, prophetic theology forms a third perspective of this proposed shape for an Old Testament theology. This perspective features prominently in the Latter Prophets—a significant portion of the Older Testament—and is thus significant in articulating the theological content of the Hebrew canon. While the Latter Prophets combine both creation and covenant dimensions of the Old Testament faith in ways that are difficult to tease apart, this section of the Old Testament has its distinctive character in the broader account of the divine-human engagement. Here the focus is on divine address of the human community, calling that community to faithful living by way of repentance. Thus, Old Testament theology consists of three legs: creation, covenant, and prophetic theologies.

Methodology

Perhaps now is a good time to return to our methodological starting point—the Psalms. I find it striking that the Psalms include a prophetic dimension—that is, a dimension comparable to the proclamation of the prophets. It is seen primarily in two places. The first is in the entrance liturgies of Psalms 15 and 24, where the qualifications for worship emphasize ethical living and thus the connection between worship and lived faith. An additional place is the prophetic warnings found in some psalms of praise. These texts include direct divine speech and call for faithful living by way of repentance (e.g., Pss. 50, 81, 82, and 95). We noted earlier Psalm 50:7, which explicitly calls for the community to hearken to God's speaking; verse 16 turns to address the wicked: "But to the wicked God says . . ." Psalm 81 concludes with a divine oracle introduced by the final line of verse 5: "I hear a voice I had not known." In Psalm 82, YHWH addresses the divine council (vv. 1, 6). The liturgical piece Psalm 95 concludes with an oracle, reflected in the last line of verse 7: "O that today you would listen to his voice!" The didactic or wisdom dimensions of the Psalter also imply a call for faithfulness, not unlike the prophetic call for faithfulness. Although not overwhelming, this prophetic dimension is clearly present and distinctive in the Psalter.

Including this third leg also reflects an eye toward the broader Old Testament. The prophetic dimension is significant in the Hebrew canon. The primogenitor of modern Psalms study, Hermann Gunkel, suggested that the prophets influenced the Psalms in the proclamation of YHWH's reign. I wonder if the reverse might well be more likely—that the prophets, growing up immersed in psalms, embraced their prophetic dimension. The prophetic is essentially theological and is a major dimension of Old Testament theology. God speaks and calls for a response of repentance.

The Psalter's cries for help and psalms of praise pulsate with creation theology, in which God is present to bless in worship and in all of life. Wisdom teaches stewardship of divine blessing. God is equally the God who comes to deliver in ancient Israel's salvation history as recited in the historical hymns and psalms of thanksgiving. That theological viewpoint undergirds the Psalter's dominant genre of lament; in these psalms the cry is for YHWH to come and deliver from crisis. So the Psalter models this tripartite organization of the faith of the Old Testament, a cogent framework for an Old Testament theology. Current Psalms scholarship suggests that the Psalter served as both hymnbook and prayer book for the ancient faith community of Israel. That is, the Psalter serves as both liturgical texts and texts for reading/meditation.[14] Beginning here in organizing an Old Testament theology suggests that

14. Bellinger, *Psalms as a Grammar for Faith*, 5, 16.

a liturgical or worshiping community provides the optimal context for constructing a theology and suggests that this theology operates on the basis of a divine-human dialogue. The central elements of human speech in the dialogue are prayer and praise.

Creation, covenant, and prophetic traditions in the Older Testament are distinct theological articulations, the goal of which is "salvation." In some Christian circles, that word is understood to be equal to deliverance, perhaps from hell to heaven or from the power of sin to the reign of God. The English word "salvation," however, comes from the Latin that indicates a life of integrity in which its various parts fit together harmoniously. Perhaps "wholeness in life" is the synonym. So in the Hebrew Scriptures, God delivers, blesses, and speaks in order to call the community and persons of faith to a life centered in the divine-human engagement, a meaningful relationship structured by *torah*, wisdom, and repentance. The goal is (abundant) life for the community and persons and the world. These texts, operating out of this tripartite shape, seek to make sense of that experience and invite readers into that reality.

Conclusion

This chapter has covered a lot of ground. It began with the conundrum that shaping an Old Testament theology brings. With such a diverse collection of ancient theological texts, how might one construct and organize a theology of the Old Testament? I have suggested a textual starting place of the Psalms as a collection of theological confessions of the ancient community who constructed the Hebrew Bible. The prayer and praise of the Psalter suggest a dialogue between human and divine as the place to begin articulating the Old Testament's word about God. The Psalms testify that God blesses, delivers, and speaks in relation to the community of faith and provides avenues of response to this divine activity. Texts of wisdom, of covenant instruction, and of prophetic calls for faithful living (repentance) articulate these paths of response. Collectively these narratives and poetic texts articulate theological dimensions we have defined as creation, covenant, and prophetic theologies. These dimensions are distinctive but also relate to each other in important ways. The goal of the three together in the Hebrew canon is "salvation" or integrity of life for the faith community and for all of creation. This goal is not limited to the ancient community; it is also relevant to today's reading communities. The narrative and poetic texts form cognitive frames and memories to shape contemporary life. Among these passages are beautiful, soaring, and inspiring texts, and also brutal and problematic texts. All of them, however, converse in the cultural memory they shape for readers and communities who seek to live in the biblical tradition. Shaping a theology of the Older Testament is complicated enough, but when we add the full hermeneutical task inherent to theology with attention to the contemporary reception of these theological texts, the task grows akin to a high-wire balancing act. The texts are nonetheless formative for persons of faith and communities of faith.

These first two chapters have set the stage for work on these theological texts of the Hebrew Scriptures. The contexts now set before us need to shape our interpretation.[15] At the same time, the normative shape of the canon calls for its part in the interpretive process. So we will proceed with a look at the parts of the Hebrew canon on the basis of the contexts set in these first two chapters. The Pentateuch is first.

---

15. Some postmodern readers will find the approach in this text a bit tame. It does not attend, for example, to much postcolonial interpretation. The postmodern is present, though, in measured ways. That is basically for hermeneutical reasons: the text is the initial point of interpretation. The movement is a conversation between text and readers guided by text rather than primarily by readers.

3

Pentateuch

The shape for an Old Testament theology this volume proposes starts with the Psalms as a textual and canonical place from which to explore ancient Israel's confessions of faith. Central to the confessions is a dialogical form that begins with revelation of the divine and provides means for humans to respond to that revelation. Based on the Psalms, I have suggested a shape for the confessions in three parts: creation, covenant, and prophetic theologies. Creation theology portrays YHWH as the one who blesses and who calls for wisdom. Covenant theology begins with God as the one who comes to deliver and who offers covenant instruction (*torah*) as a means of response. Prophetic theology characterizes the divine revelation in terms of the God who speaks and the anticipated human response as repentance. These three dimensions confess faith in YHWH, who seeks wholeness of life for ancient Israel, for all the nations, and for all creation. We will proceed to explore this theology by way of attention to the parts of the Protestant canon. We will not structure the study by the three legs of the tripos but will explore these dimensions as we work our way through the sections of the Hebrew canon. The Pentateuch or Torah is the first section.

The Torah consists of the first five books of the Bible, books that pass down the tradition of the Mosaic covenant and so are often labeled the books of Moses. The metanarrative of these texts suggests that the first book, Genesis, focuses on creation theology, while the remaining books focus on covenant theology, though these two dimensions intertwine. A central interpretive issue is how Genesis relates with the four books that follow. My goal is not to summarize the various parts of these texts but to explore their theological shape.

Creation Theology in Genesis

The two large sections of Genesis are the primeval history (Gen. 1–11) and the ancestral narratives (Gen. 12–50). The primeval history (history of the first age) begins with two creation accounts and then recounts scenes of the beginnings of human history, fitting for a book entitled "Origins."

Primeval History

Most interpreters agree that the litany in Genesis 1 and the narrative in Genesis 2–3 constitute two creation accounts. In addition to the differences in genre, the creation begins differently and the names and portrayals of God are rather different in the two accounts. The order of creation and the place of humans in it also differ. Both accounts are in these first chapters of Genesis. The accounts are not understood as contradictory but as providing two different perspectives on creation, one from the broad angle of the whole and one from the narrower angle of the narrative setting in the garden of Eden.

The primeval history continues with two literary genres: genealogies and narratives. The genealogies list the generations (Gen. 5; 10; 11). The genealogies add people to the brief narratives and show the divine blessing flowing through the generations leading to Abram and Sarai and their descendants. Although often ignored by contemporary readers, the genealogies are in some sense the glue that holds together the narratives in Genesis 1–11 and pushes the plot forward. These genealogies continue the orderliness of creation from Genesis 1.

Genesis 1

The first chapter of Genesis reads like a worship litany and portrays Elohim as creating the world effortlessly by speaking it into existence. The account is organized according to seven days culminating with God pronouncing a blessing on all of creation. Its structure strongly emphasizes man and woman as created in the image of God (see table 2).

This most familiar of the creation texts in the Hebrew Scriptures has brought many theological reflections. It is not possible in this context to deal with all the issues raised. Four, however, are central to the text.

In the Image of God

As table 2 suggests, the emphasis of this finely tuned litany is in day 6 and especially in the creation of humans in the divine image. This part of God's creating is emphasized thrice in verse 27:

> So God created humankind in his image,
> in the image of God he created them;
> male and female he created them.

And it is followed by the divine blessing and authorization in verse 28. Much ink has been spilled over attempts to define the image of God. The vocabulary of "image" and "likeness" brings to mind royal statuary in the ancient Near East where statues symbolized the ruler's survey and rule over the kingdom. Rather than setting up royal statues, God creates women and men as representatives of the divine.[1] God reigns over the creation, and humans represent God in taking care of (ruling over) the earth and its inhabitants. Most English translations use the language of "having dominion" over the earth and all of its creatures; the sense of the term reflects the ruler's task of caring for

---

1. Von Rad, *Old Testament Theology*, 1:144–48.

Table 2. Literary Structure of Genesis 1

Tohu (Unformed)	*Bohu* (Unfilled)
Day 1 (Gen. 1:3–5)	**Day 4 (1:14–19)**
Divine command (1:3–5a)	Divine command (1:14–18)
Appearance of light (1:3)	The command (1:14–15)
Division of light from darkness (1:4)	Command that lights appear
Naming of night and day (1:5a)	(1:14a)
Summary phrase (1:5b)	Purposes of the lights (1:14b–15)
	Execution of the command (1:16–18)
	Making the lights (1:16)
	Their purposes fulfilled (1:17–18)
	Summary phrase (1:19)
Day 2 (1:6–8)	**Day 5 (1:20–23)**
Divine command (1:6–8a)	Divine command (1:20–22)
Making of sky (1:6–7a)	Command to produce fish and birds
Division of lower waters from	(1:20)
upper (1:7b)	Resultant creation of fish and birds
Naming of heaven (1:8a)	(1:21)
Summary phrase (1:8b)	Blessing of fish and birds (1:22)
	Summary phrase (1:23)
Day 3 (1:9–13)	**Day 6 (1:24–31)**
Two divine commands (1:9–12)	Three divine commands (1:24–30)
Command one (1:9–10)	Command one (1:24–25)
Division of lower waters from dry	Command to produce earth
land (1:9)	creatures (1:24)
Naming of earth and seas (1:10)	Resultant production of earth
Command two (1:11–12)	creatures (1:25)
Command to produce vegeta-	Command two (1:26–28)
tion (1:11)	Decision to make humanity (1:26)
Resultant production of vegeta-	Resultant creation thrice
tion (1:12)	emphasized (1:27)
Summary phrase (1:13)	Blessing of humanity (1:28)
	Command three: Provision of
	vegetation as food (1:29–30)
	Summary phrase (1:31)

Source: Chart adapted from Arterbury, Bellinger, and Dodson, *Engaging the Christian Scriptures*, 32. See also Brueggemann and Linafelt, *Introduction to the Old Testament*, 54–59; Collins, *Short Introduction to the Hebrew Bible*, 36–42, 45–46.

the kingdom and all dwelling in it. Verses 26 and 28 emphasize this functional understanding of humans as the image of God.

The vocabulary suggests also that humans are not God. An image or likeness is not the original but rather a reflection of the original. At the same time, the image has a connection to the original, and so humans can respond to the divine and relate to the divine. The divine-human encounter underlies the understanding of female and male created in the image of God. Both male and female are created in the image of God and relate to God. The divine-human encounter is essential to biblical understandings of both the divine and the human and so is part of the context of this opening chapter of the Hebrew Bible.

Ancient Near Eastern Context

The creation account in Genesis 1 is often compared to the Babylonian Enuma Elish. There are similarities in the sequence and organization of these two creation accounts. Genesis 1 naturally reflects the cultural codes of the context from which it comes. This revelation of the creator Elohim is part of the sociohistorical world of ancient Israel. The plural references to God in 1:26 ("Let us make humankind in our image, according to our likeness") also likely reflect this background of the text. The portrayal is of a divine king who speaks to the council of the Lord, the messengers gathered in the divine throne room. The divine name Elohim is also a plural form, perhaps reflecting all of the divine functions of the various ancient Near Eastern deities in ancient Israel's one deity. The God revealed in this text is involved in the life that God and human beings have together, their history.

The sociocultural background of the text is reflected therein, but the text still makes clear the theological perspective of the living God of ancient Israel. Genesis 1, for example, is more peaceful and orderly as a creation account, and the place of humans in the biblical text is clearly enhanced by their being the image of God. Whereas the Babylonian text includes various gods and goddesses, the final word in Genesis 1 is that Elohim, the living God of the faith community of ancient Israel, is the creator; the community should not be confused by the deities of all the peoples around them. The conclusion of this opening creation account (2:1–4) makes clear that the Sabbath is for worship of the one God who creates and lives.

The Creating God Who Blesses

Genesis 1 is the most familiar piece of creation theology in the Older Testament and sets the stage for all that follows. This text of creation theology portrays God as the one who blesses, whose hovering spirit makes it possible to grow and thrive in the world. God is present to bless the sea creatures and the birds (v. 22) and humans as those created in the divine image (v. 28). "God blessed them, and God said to them, 'Be fruitful and multiply, and fill the earth and subdue it; and have dominion over the fish of the sea and over the birds of the air and over every living thing that moves on the earth.'" God provides for life.

The introduction (1:1–2) and conclusion (2:1–3) of this account also support this understanding of God as the one who is present to bless in this opening creation account. The powerful spirit or wind of God hovers over the face of the deep like a mother bird in 1:2. The ordering of creation finds its conclusion in making the Sabbath holy as a time of worship and rest. "So God blessed the seventh day and hallowed it" (2:3). This seven-day account is formative for the creation theology witnessed to in the rest of the Hebrew Scriptures.

A Priestly Perspective

Most Old Testament scholars would agree that this creation account is part of the Priestly writing in the Pentateuch.[2] Its connections with worship, order, and blessing fit with other Priestly texts and concerns. Most scholars would associate the Priestly writing with the experience of exile and its aftermath in one way or another. So Genesis 1 is about more than understandings of creation or nature in the abstract. The authorization to "be fruitful and multiply, and fill the earth" could also apply to the return from defeat and exile to encounter the divine blessing to fill the land again, to order life again and begin anew.

---

2. See Smith, *Priestly Vision of Genesis 1*; Brueggemann, "Kerygma of the Priestly Writer."

The word *'erets* may be translated "earth" or "land," depending on the context. The creation account in Genesis 1 is also about God's blessing presence for a community who has suffered forced migration and oppression and now is called to grow and thrive in the blessing of God's creation.

It is likely that the first sentence of 2:4 ("These are the generations of the heavens and the earth when they were created") also comes from those responsible for the Priestly creation account, placed here as an introduction to what follows. Genesis 1 introduces the whole of the Older Testament, and now the narrative of God in relation to the creation will continue in telling of the "generations of the heavens and the earth." The angle of vision narrows from universal to a garden.

Genesis 2–3

Genesis 2–3 tells the story of the garden of Eden. This text has a different feel and literary style than does Genesis 1. God is portrayed in anthropomorphic terms, like a human. First comes the land and then the divine potter makes *'adam* from the dust of the ground (*'adamah*). The garden is filled with plants and trees. The animals are then created, and the search for human community leads to the creation of a woman as the mother of all living things. The man and the woman are entrusted with care of the garden.

Among the trees planted in the garden is the tree of the knowledge of good and evil, and the man and the woman are prohibited from eating of the fruit of that tree. Genesis 3 pursues the reality of the prohibition as the serpent, who is simply characterized as craftier (a wisdom term) than the other animals, tempts the woman to break the prohibition, which she and the man do. Consequently, the pair is expelled from the garden. The theological dimensions of this narrative are many indeed.

Sin and the Order of Creation

This narrative recounts in a lively way the beauty and the troubles in the beginnings of a universal human history. At the center of an overabundance of theological meaning is the problem of the man and woman's breaking of the prohibition. In Protestant tradition, this narrative is central for exploring the Old Testament's understanding of sin. In this narrative, sin is the attempt to take the place of God. God is the creator, who gives life. Here the man and woman succumb to the temptation to usurp the place of the creator and change the order of life, breaking the prohibition given as part of the order of creation. They have become like God, knowing good and evil, a phrase that may well be a way of saying "knowing all things." The phrase also connotes connections with wisdom.

In this creation theology, God acts as the creator who blesses, who gives all the gifts for full living. Included in the gifts is the prohibition about ordering life. The task of the humans is to live this life with wisdom, learning to live according to the created order. The breaking of the prohibition is an act of folly resulting in expulsion from the garden and a life of troubles. The narrative is a tantalizing account of the blessing God in creation and the fraught call to respond wisely in living. The story becomes a cautionary tale. This narrative makes known that from the very beginning, humans have gotten things wrong and broken the order of creation. The consequences encompass all of creation.

The Human Creation

In 2:7, when the Lord forms the man, the text indicates that the Lord breathes into the man the breath of life and the man becomes a living *nephesh*. The term is often taken to mean that the man has a soul in the traditional connotation of that English phrase. But the text says not that the man *has* a soul but that the man *becomes* a living soul, a person, a living being, a self: "Then the LORD God formed man from the dust of the ground, and breathed into his nostrils the breath of life; and the man became a living being." The verse also associates humans (*'adam*) with the ground (*'adamah*) from which they come.

This holistic view of the human pervades the biblical tradition and suggests that the life of each person includes all the perspectives of humans one can imagine—physical, spiritual, intellectual, artistic, imaginative, social, and more. This integrated view of persons suggests that the created order embraces all those aspects of living and with them the inherent complexity of a life-embracing creation. This text celebrates all the possibilities for human life in God's creation but also cautions us to observe the limits that persist in human life. The prohibition is important in the narrative.

Human Relationships in Creation

Genesis 1–3 is a crucial set of texts regarding relations of women and men. Genesis 1:27 makes clear that man and woman are both created in the image of God. In the narrative of Genesis 2–3, it is clear that woman and man are essential to the continuing search for human community and to the centrality of human community to the fulfillment of creation. The man and the woman are closely connected as human partners and are to care for the garden, and both are involved in the sufferings of life. It is clear that both the woman and the man are to help each other and so are understood to be equal and connected partners.[3]

This narrative begins with the idyllic creation account of the garden of Eden with the animals and the man and woman in full community. Chapter 3, however, recounts the breaking of the prohibition that was part of the created order and the consequences of that sin. In the initial prohibition in 2:17, the consequence of the sin is death. The serpent denies that the woman and man will die. The two do not die in the most common sense of that word, but a number of theologians have suggested that they die spiritually—that is, their relationships with God and with each other are broken in that act of denying the created order. While Genesis 3 focuses on the sin and its consequences for all of creation, the man and the woman ultimately receive the gift of continuing the human experience outside the garden. God also graciously clothes them before they leave (3:21).

---

3. The Hebrew Bible comes from a patriarchal culture, but in these creation texts, it is fair to say, as this paragraph suggests, that God is not gendered.

Additional Narratives in Genesis 4–11

Three additional narratives follow in the primeval history. Genesis 4 recounts the story of the next generation—Cain and Abel, the sons of the man and woman from the garden (Adam and Eve). Cain reacts badly when God accepts Abel's sacrifice, killing his brother in a violent act of sin. God's confrontation with Cain leads to punishment in the form of Cain's banishment from his clan (v. 12). Genesis 6–9 recounts the story of Noah and the flood.[4] Genesis 6 makes it clear that the flood is a response to the evil that has now pervaded the human community. Chapter 9 tells the story of the renewal of the relationship between God and all creation, reflecting the language of the Priestly creation account in Genesis 1 with the blessing of Noah and his family to "be fruitful and multiply and fill the earth." There is a future for the human community. The language of blessing is central in this remarkable narrative, as are priestly acts of worship, but the language of covenant is also part of the picture; the two are enmeshed. The final narrative in the primeval history is the story of the tower of Babel in Genesis 11.[5] In its context in the primeval history, the story is about ongoing human efforts to take the place of God. Human sin continues after the flood, as indicated in this story and also in the latter part of Genesis 9 in Noah's family.

Theological Shape of the Primeval History Narratives

What is the theological import of the primeval history narratives? The narratives of the garden of Eden, of Cain and Abel, of Noah and the flood, and of the tower of Babel all follow a pattern of disobedience against God and the consequences thereof (see table 3).

The divine-human relationship is embodied in human relationships. However, the narratives end not with the consequences of a broken

---

4. This flood narrative has parallels in other flood narratives in the ancient Near East. These narratives in the primeval history come from a cultural context and reflect that, as well as contributing their distinctive perspectives.

5. Most interpreters suggest that the story originated as an etiology for the presence of many nations and languages and that it reflects Babylonian culture with the allusion to ziggurats in the tower and with the association of the name Babel with the verb meaning "to confuse."

Table 3. Narrative Structure of Genesis 2–11

Narrative	Sin	Punishment	Grace
Genesis 2–3: Garden of Eden	Eating the fruit	Expulsion	Clothes/life
Genesis 4: Cain and Abel	Murder	Ostracism	Mark of protection
Genesis 6–9: Noah and the flood	Pervasive sin	Flood	Noah/ark
Genesis 11: Tower of Babel	Storming heaven	Dispersion/ confusion	?

Source: Adapted from Arterbury, Bellinger, and Dodson, Engaging the Christian Scriptures, 36.

relationship but rather with an act of grace in the divine-human relationship. The sequence of the narratives is sin-punishment-grace.

The dominant theme is the growing power of sin, and the counter-theme is the growing power of grace in the world. In the face of a broken creation, the creator subtly continues to support blessing and hope. The fourth narrative, that of the tower of Babel, raises questions at the end of this first major section of the Hebrew Bible. The narrative suggests that creation is still in travail, but where is the sense of hope? A number of interpreters suggest that the sign of grace comes in the call of Abram and Sarai.[6] So the first major section of Genesis begins with the divine ordering and blessing of both creation and the human community. Although troubled on account of human folly, both continue and are not without hope in the divine blessing. Can the human community discover and pass on the wisdom to live fully in the face of the folly that has lurked at the door, even in the hope of the creator's blessing and provision for wholeness of life together?

Ancestral Narratives

The genealogy that concludes Genesis 11 introduces the family of Abram and Sarai, the central characters at the outset of the second major division of Genesis. The narrative now shifts away from the

6. See von Rad, *Old Testament Theology*, 1:163–64; von Rad, "Form-Critical Problem of the Hexateuch," 65–67; Clines, *Theme of the Pentateuch*, 85–86; Wolff, "Kerygma of the Yahwist."

universal history of Genesis 1–11 to focus on a family history of the first fathers (patriarchs) and first mothers (matriarchs) of the Hebrew people. The text covers four generations beginning with Abram and Sarai.

The Covenant Promise of Blessing

From the universal perspective of the primeval history, the narrative narrows to focus on this family, beginning with the call of Abram, and yet the theme of sin-punishment-grace persists. This continuing divine initiative in relating to humans provides the act of divine kindness that was missing from Genesis 11.

The introductory preface (12:1–3) to the ancestral narratives is a crucial sign of the significance of the stories to come. God calls Abram to leave home and family and go "to the land that I will show you." Along with this imperative to go comes the ancestral covenant promise of blessing, often put in terms of descendants, land, and blessing. While the promise is often characterized in covenant language, the text anticipates divine blessing and presence to empower growth and thriving in the world. The purpose of this blessing is not simply that those who are blessed may enjoy a good life but that they may bring the blessing to "all the families of the earth." The focus narrows to one family, but as a means of blessing for all of creation. The whole of creation is never far from the election of this one Hebrew family. This ancestral covenant promise of blessing is the primary theological theme of the ancestral narratives in Genesis. The theme is renewed in all four generations of the ancestors (15:5–7; 17:2, 7, 19, 21; 26:24; 28:3–4, 13–15; 48:16). The intriguing literature of Genesis always seems to have a countertheme to push the narrative forward. In this case, the counter is the threats that arise to the promise: Will it continue?

The means of response to the creator's blessing is found in wisdom for living. The abilities of Abram and Sarai to make their way in the creation and to lean into the divine blessing indicate wisdom. Even Jacob's trickery suggests wisdom for living in the blessing of this life of wandering. And Joseph's wisdom enriches and shares the divine blessing with those in need. Full wisdom comes in trusting the divine blessing as the basis for a whole life. Learning—that is, growth in wisdom—comes in the face of difficulties.

Threats to Blessing

Threats that arise include barrenness in the face of the promise of progeny (Gen. 16); the matriarchs in danger, for the blessing is also tied to them (12:10–20); sibling rivalry between Jacob and Esau (Gen. 27); and conflicts with locals (Gen. 34). Threats to the future of the promise are central to the story of the Joseph generation as well, such as the jealousy of the brothers, Joseph's conflict related to Potiphar's wife, and famine.

Barrenness

Since the promise of blessing requires progeny, the provision of a first child is a major plot point for the text. Ancient stories often deal with the difficulty of barrenness, since a future is found in the generations. Genesis 12:2 promises that Abram ("exalted ancestor") will become a great nation, having many descendants. His name becomes Abraham, "ancestor of a multitude" (17:5). And so a descendant is necessary. The repetition of the promise in the covenant ceremony in Genesis 15 speaks to the centrality of the promise of a child. As Sarai's barrenness persists, she suggests they follow one of the cultural customs of the day and gives Abram her servant, who bears Ishmael. Abram and Sarai must come to the wisdom that the promise is to come from Sarai as well as Abram, and that promise is repeated as a covenant promise in Genesis 17. It is a crooked pilgrimage Abraham and Sarah take with the divine promise, but the divine keeps coming to them to remind them of the promise of blessing. And Sarah and Abraham give birth to Isaac. Wise living for them was to come to trust the promise. Yet God also provided a future for Ishmael. The famous text of Genesis 22 and the command to offer Isaac as a sacrifice also centers on the interplay between the promise of blessing of a descendant and learning to trust in the promise giver (22:15–19). Rebecca was also barren but gave birth in due time to twins (25:21–22) following Isaac's prayer. Rachel in the next generation struggled also with barrenness. Her sister Leah provides sons for Jacob, as do the servants of both wives. In all these cases, the blessing of birth is tied to divine presence with both father and mothers of these children. Finally, Rachel receives the blessing of a child (30:22–24). The God who blesses with descendants continues to journey with this extended family and to bless them with progeny. That blessing comes to pass in the natural order of life, a basic understanding of wisdom theology. The community works to learn that order of life and to live by it.

Matriarchs in Danger

Sarah (twice: Gen. 12 and 20) and Rebecca (Gen. 26) experience remarkably similar dangers, and since the covenant blessing is to come through the matriarchs, these encounters threaten the promise. In chapter 12, Abram seeks to pass off Sarai as his sister rather than his wife. He fears that the Egyptians will kill him to take his beautiful wife. When Sarai is taken into the pharaoh's house, Abram receives considerable wealth. Plagues come on the pharaoh's house, and they are understood as judgment from God. The pharaoh confronts Abram about his wife Sarai. God is present to preserve Sarai and Abram and the promise in this story that includes the theme of household wealth.

Sibling Rivalry

Sibling rivalry often breaks out between the twins Jacob and Esau and between Joseph and his brothers. The conflict between the twins has to do with blessing and the carrying of the covenant promise into the future. In chapter 27, Rebecca manipulates Jacob into taking the blessing from his brother Esau by deceiving their aged father. Jacob receives the blessing tied to the divine blessing, and Esau angrily yearns for that blessing. This scene of family conflict and blessing leads Jacob to his uncle's house in Haran where he marries Leah and Rachel. On the journey, Jacob encounters God at Bethel, and God speaks to him the covenant promise of blessing for this community. In all these stories, the material blessing of household wealth is important in the story. The blessing and name of the family grows. This blessing is a sign of wisdom.

Conflict with Locals

The story of Joseph's generation focuses on several threats to the covenant promise—famine, sibling rivalry, and conflicts with local citizens. In chapter 34, Shechem, the son of a local politician, rapes Jacob's daughter Dinah and then seeks to bargain with Jacob's family to give him Dinah as a wife. Jacob's sons trick the townsmen of Shechem into circumcision and then fall upon them and slaughter them. They take the wealth of Shechem. The chapter is an odd story, but it likely reflects the dangers the family of Jacob faced in its journeys and illustrates their taking of household wealth. The Joseph story illustrates conflict with the Egyptian people after Joseph is sold into Egypt by his brothers. He ends up in prison, but as an example of a wise character, he finds his way to remarkable power. He interprets dreams, embodies the characteristics of wisdom in Proverbs, and comes to a position in which he wisely provides food for many people, including his own family. His wisdom comes from the creator; it is blessing Joseph must learn to trust, and it becomes a means of growing to be a great nation.

The conflict between the promise and threats to the promise drives the narratives and helps readers follow the import of the stories. Genesis 12:1–3 signals the theme of blessing so integral for interpreting this latter part of Genesis. In the end (50:20), the book concludes with the promise intact.

Concluding Thoughts on Genesis and Creation Theology

These latter chapters of Genesis portray God as the one who blesses, the one who makes it possible for the heirs to the promise to grow and thrive in everyday life. That theological portrayal fits with the characterization of Joseph as a wise person who embodies the characteristics of wisdom in Proverbs. He interprets dreams and perceives ways into the future of the ancestral covenant promise in this Egyptian setting.

He becomes a character who models a wise way of life for the young in ancient Israel.[7] The divine revelation is the promise of blessing the order of life, and Joseph embodies the human response. The Joseph cycle—and the rest of the ancestral narratives—may well read like a soap opera to many contemporary readers, but the metanarrative focuses on the God who blesses (that is, the creator). Genesis as a whole reveals a God who orders life in a variety of contexts. God is present to bring the power to grow and thrive in life fraught with threat and with breaks in the order of creation. This God grants the gift of wisdom to discover ways forward for the future of the community. This blessing is for not only this community but also, through this community, all creation. Genesis begins with the broadest angle of vision, viewing God's creation of the world and its inhabitants. It focuses in chapter 12 on one family and its descendants, but the broad hope for all of creation never leaves. By way of divine providence, at the end of the book of Genesis, the hope for blessing remains intact.

Covenant Theology in Exodus

The opening paragraph of Exodus actually alludes to Genesis 1 and its creation theology. The sons of Jacob have been fruitful, multiplied, and filled the land. The people have become a great nation; now comes the land. This paragraph also introduces the transition to the narrative of the people in Egypt and their exodus from oppression there. In the first half of Exodus, covenant takes center stage, with the faith community's cry for help in Egyptian bondage, the divine hearing of the cry, and God's coming to liberate the community. The exodus from Egypt leads to the creation of the covenant community and instruction (*torah*) in how to live in that relationship. Following the agreement of the covenant relationship, Exodus moves to instruction in worship for the faith community. God hears their lament and comes to deliver and, in so doing, creates a covenant community and provides instruc-

7. Von Rad, "The Joseph Narrative and Ancient Wisdom."

tion for it. Central to that instruction is worship as human response to divine revelation.

God Hears a Lament and Comes to Deliver

Exodus 3 is a central text for Old Testament covenant theology focused on YHWH who hears the cry of lament from the Hebrews oppressed in Egypt and comes to deliver. Moses is here called to bring about this deliverance, and he understandably asks for the name of this God who is calling him to this overwhelming task. The answer is the revelation of the divine name YHWH in verses 14–15: "God said to Moses, 'I AM WHO I AM.' He said further, 'Thus you shall say to the Israelites, "I AM has sent me to you."' God also said to Moses, 'Thus you shall say to the Israelites, "The LORD, the God of your ancestors, the God of Abraham, the God of Isaac, and the God of Jacob, has sent me to you."'"

The phrase can be reasonably translated "I am who I am," "I am what I am," or "I will be what I will be." It associates the name with the Hebrew verb meaning "to be," suggesting that this God is the one who brings things into being and, in the context of Exodus 3, who will come to deliver this people from bondage in Egypt. The phrase also suggests that this God is not one who will be manipulated. The divine name is associated with the ancestors of Genesis. This dialogue of the Holy One with Moses establishes God's authority to call Moses to deliver God's people. The emphasis is on this holy God who has heard the groans of the people and will come to deliver them, even though the task is perplexing to Moses.

The account of the conflict leading to the deliverance of the Hebrews from Egyptian slavery centers on the plagues, a series of progressively intensifying mighty acts that establish the authority of YHWH for both Israel and Egypt and bring Pharaoh to release Israel from bondage. The plagues assert that YHWH is above all gods, not shaken by magic, and not equaled by any power (9:14). In these narratives, YHWH defeats Egyptian gods and goddesses such as the god of the Nile, insect deities, Hathor, Ra, and Ptah. This section powerfully establishes YHWH as both creator and deliverer. The final plague of the death of the firstborn brings about the release of the captives from oppression. The festival of Passover establishes the community's memory of this deliverance and the community's protection from death. This narrative is central to ancient Israel's faith. It continues with the crossing of the sea on dry ground and the demise of the Egyptian army pursuing the Hebrews.

This narrative in the first half of Exodus is the paradigmatic memory of God as the one who hears the cry of those in need and comes to deliver. Exodus 3 narrates the heart of covenant theology in the Pentateuch. At the Sea of Reeds, YHWH uses the power of the wind to bring Israel across and to destroy the Egyptian oppressors (14:21–31). This YHWH who delivers is also creator, the one who controls the wind, who gives and takes life in the plague of the firstborn. Both theological perspectives are clear and present. Additionally, God makes powerful use of human power in this account, as reflected in the reference to Moses in 14:31. The leadership of Moses is a central part of the story. Women also play a significant role in this paradigmatic liberation narrative in ancient Israel—Moses's mother, Jochebed; Moses's sister, Miriam (called a prophet); Moses's wife, Zipporah; Pharaoh's daughter; and the midwives Shiphrah and Puah. Human participation in divine deliverance is frequently important in Old Testament covenant theology narratives. The center of these narratives is the mighty acts that accomplish YHWH's purposes for the community of ancient Israel. YHWH effects deliverance by various means.

Yet the narrative makes clear that the conclusion of the story does not come with the release of the captives but moves on to the making of a covenant relationship between Yahweh and Israel. The ongoing memory of this narrative centers in worship, in the Festival of Passover and in the extraordinary psalm of Miriam/Moses in Exodus 15 celebrating God's defeat of the oppressive Egyptian army. The psalm both expresses the community's faith and joy and interprets these events for the community and its descendants. This deliverance of the Hebrews is seen as a mighty act of God to create a community of worshipers in covenant with YHWH. The Passover liturgy and the psalm keep the congregation of Israel singing and remembering in their life together.

God Creates a Community and Provides Covenant Instruction (Torah)

The deliverance from Egyptian oppression leads to an extension of the paradigm in the theophany at Sinai and to the founding of the covenant relationship between YHWH and ancient Israel as a faith community. In Exodus 20 YHWH reveals the shape of life for Israel as the covenant people of YHWH, beginning with the focus of such a life in the Decalogue or Ten Words. Divine revelation leads to human response. The first commandment comes in verse 3. The two preceding verses set the context in terms of divine revelation from the one who has delivered this people out of bondage in Egypt. These commandments articulate life for this community in relationship with this covenant-making God YHWH. The first table of the Decalogue envisions the shape of life with YHWH, and the second table with one another. The Decalogue integrates worship and ethical living. The list of ten is central to the covenant relationship. It is built on the relationship with the living God YHWH and enacting that relationship in the life of the community. It embodies ancient Israel's life together as the focus of the worshiping community. The form of these commandments is apodictic, giving basic universal instruction based on the authority of the lawgiver, YHWH, who delivered this community from bondage. Following the Decalogue comes the Covenant Code in 20:22–23:19. This law code is mostly casuistic in form (composed of case law), expanding the Decalogue and applying it to daily life for ancient Israel. After these law codes have been stated in the narrative, YHWH and Israel enter into this covenant relationship.

These law codes are often neglected in contemporary faith circles. When they are discussed, they are often interpreted in a way that confirms the stereotype of YHWH as a harsh, judgmental deity. These texts are set in the context of divine revelation, already a different context than contemporary legal material with which most Western readers are familiar. "Law" in the Older Testament carries three connotations:

1. A means of response to the divine deliverance from Egyptian bondage
2. A revelation of the shape of life in a covenant community
3. A means of deepening relationship—with YHWH and with fellow members of the covenant community

Covenant does not begin with law but with divine initiative in a gracious deliverance of this oppressed people. That act leads to faithful human response, and so a relationship emerges and grows for the community. The term usually translated "law" is *torah*. Better renderings are "instruction," "teaching," "guidance," or "direction." *Torah* is not a piece of government legislation, nor is it a means of earning divine favor. *Torah* is a gift, divine revelation of the shape of life together as a covenant community. The community does not live by *torah* in order to become the people of YHWH, but rather because they already are the people of YHWH, they live by *torah*. They became the covenant community linked to YHWH when they were delivered from oppression in Egypt. The structure of the beginning of the Decalogue in Exodus 20 makes this point clearly. Because of Israel's identity as the covenant community, they live in a certain way, the way of *torah*. A full rendering of the term would be "covenant instruction." The instruction is desiccated when it is divorced from the covenant-making narrative, emphasizing a relationship initiated by YHWH. Covenant is a way of understanding the relationship between YHWH and Israel in which YHWH declares, "I will be your God," and Israel responds, "We will be your people." YHWH initiates this connection and teaches the people how to live as the covenant community (*torah*). The response of the community in living out the relationship carries consequences. The narrative of the first half of Exodus provides the context for this covenant relationship that is determinative for Israel's identity and purpose. This covenant theology of the God who comes to deliver and the means of response in *torah* is the theological center of Exodus and is essential to much of the Older Testament. Note that this covenant relationship is dialogical. God hears the lament of the suffering community and comes to deliver. Continuing to speak such laments in a broken world and continuing to recite and enact this covenant-creating story in worship and faith are central to the nurturing of the covenant relationship.

Instruction for Worship as Human Response to Divine Revelation

The latter half of Exodus focuses on the place of worship and ritual in the covenant between YHWH and Israel. Worship is essential to the human response to the divine initiative. The academic term for the community's organized worship is "cult." Cultic matters are central for a community whose life is shaped by a relationship with a deity. Some will find the seemingly endless details of these chapters to be boring relics of a long-forgotten past, but these matters were at the heart of life for the Priestly theologians who shaped these texts and passed them on. The theological perspectives woven into the text continue to shape life in the divine-human relationship.

The confirming of the covenant relationship in Exodus 24 centers on worship. Chapters 25–40 continue this emphasis on worship with a lengthy account of the tabernacle's construction. The mobile sanctuary will be the place where the divine presence can travel with the covenant community, so detailed instructions are provided for its construction and for how priests must preside over worship within it. After sixteen chapters, the tabernacle is finally built and accepted as a worthy place of worship in the final paragraph of the book (40:34–38). The divine presence "tabernacles" there.

Tucked in these cultic building plans is a text rich with theological import—29:43–46. This divine speech takes place at the entrance to the tabernacle, called the tent of meeting, the place where YHWH meets with Moses as the covenant mediator: "I will meet with the Israelites there, and it shall be sanctified by my glory; I will consecrate the tent of meeting and the altar; Aaron also and his sons I will consecrate, to serve me as priests. I will dwell among the Israelites, and I will be their God. And they shall know that I am the LORD their God, who brought them out of the land of Egypt that I might dwell among them; I am the LORD their God." It is the covenant relationship between YHWH and Israel initiated with the deliverance from oppression in Egypt that brings about this extensive articulation of the cultic order. The divine presence makes possible wholeness of life for ancient Israel, and the tabernacle cult makes it possible for YHWH to continue to be present with this community. Divine revelation leads to human response in worship.

Covenant and Creation Theologies in Leviticus

Leviticus centers on the presence of YHWH with this faith community. YHWH delivered this people from slavery and established it as a covenant community. The *torah* this book articulates teaches the people the proper response. There is no one like YHWH, and the worshiping community is to respond by living in a distinct way—that is, to embody the divine holiness or distinctiveness—and the book instructs in how to do that. The book also understands that the relationship with YHWH and relationships among humans can be fractured by sin and uncleanness. Instruction in sacrifice and in cleansing rituals makes it possible to repair such fractures. All of this instruction (*torah*) is a gift from the covenant God YHWH given at Sinai for this community that has been delivered from bondage in Egypt and called to be a priestly and holy people (Exod. 19:6).

Instruction for Sacrifices as Human Response to Divine Revelation

The Priestly emphasis on worship continues in Leviticus, most of which is taken up with codes associated with worship in the form of sacrifices. Before sacrifices can be offered, there must be instruction for both priests and other members of the community. Thus, the book begins with the Manual of Sacrifice both for those bringing sacrifices (1:1–6:7) and for the priests who administer them (6:8–7:38). The opening chapters delineate five types of sacrifices:

1. The whole burnt offering, an atoning sacrifice in which one offers the whole of life to YHWH (Lev. 1)
2. The cereal offering, marking that everyday life is a gift from God (Lev. 2)
3. The shared offering, in which both YHWH and worshipers share in the sacrificial meal (Lev. 3)
4. The purification offering, for the purpose of cleansing from the effects of sin and uncleanness (4:1–5:13)
5. The compensation offering, which makes reparations for guilt (5:14–6:7)

Such sacrificial rituals seem foreign to many contemporary readers. These rituals are not mechanical or legalistic in the literary context of Leviticus but are significant expressions of covenant theology. They are genuine acts of faith in several ways, human responses to divine initiative. The cereal offering, for example, gives thanks to YHWH for the provisions for life. The shared offering nurtures communion between the covenant community and the covenant God. In other cases, the sacrifice serves the purpose of atonement, putting back "at one" the relationship with the covenant God and other members of the covenant community. The character of at-one-ment sacrifices has been an issue of considerable debate. Some have characterized such sacrifices in less than positive terms, as means of currying favor with the deity or bribing an angry deity. In the context of Leviticus, the best account suggests that the ritual provides a setting for communication between worshipers and deity. The worshiper who brings and identifies with the sacrifice risks taking the life of the sacrificial animal, a creature who rightfully belongs to God. The deity mysteriously honors that risk and wipes clean the divine-human relationship, putting it back "at one."

Such Priestly texts assume that sin and uncleanness break the relationship of the covenant God and the worshiping community; sacrifice is the divinely given means of repairing this life-giving relationship and making it possible for the deity to continue to tabernacle with Israel and give it wholeness of life. Sacrifice embodies a human response to the divine initiative of delivering and creating this covenant community.

Creation Theology as Basis for Ritual Purity

While Exodus mainly employs covenant theology, Leviticus weaves in elements of creation theology as well. This perspective is seen most explicitly in chapters 11–15, the Manual of Purity or instruction in what is clean and unclean. Definitions are central in these chapters. "Clean" is not a comment on whether one is "dirty" but on what is acceptable for worship; that which is "unclean" is unacceptable for worship, and uncleanness is contagious. Exclusion from worship in this covenant community is destructive and so to be avoided. The reasons for exclusion are delineated in order to avoid such exclusion. The manual covers eating unclean food (Lev. 11), bleeding in childbirth (Lev. 12), contracting scaly skin diseases (Lev. 13–14), and encountering bodily emissions (Lev. 15). There have been a variety of attempts to account for these reasons for impurity. Some would emphasize obedience to the covenant God or health concerns or the need to distinguish this covenant community from other communities. It seems likely that underlying these instructions is connection with the Priestly creation theology portrayed in Genesis 1 and related to a variety of life settings. Genesis 1 portrays an orderly creation, and the Manual of Purity gives further instruction in responding to that revelation on how to live fully in that ordered creation. All the specifics are not clear, but the context emphasizes the provision of instruction in how to prepare to engage in worship of the life-giving covenant God.

Preparation for worship is also reflected in the narrative in Leviticus 16 concerning the Day of Atonement, a ritual that cleanses impurity. Both the priest and tabernacle are cleansed of sin and impurity. The cleansing of the tabernacle makes it possible for the completely holy YHWH to continue to be present in the sanctuary at the center of the covenant community and to give life to the people. This ritual suggests that Priestly theology understands that sin and uncleanness can fracture the divine-human relationship as well as relationships within the covenant community. The ritual provides a way to renew and restore the relationship. Worship nurtures the covenant relationship between YHWH and Israel. The Manual of Purity and the Day of Atonement ritual work to ensure that worship continues for the life of the covenant community.

Instructions for Holiness as Human Response to Divine Revelation

Leviticus 17–26 is often characterized as the Holiness Code, based on the frequently occurring language that instructs Israel to be holy as YHWH is holy.[8] The concern is that the covenant community will live and worship reflecting the divine holiness as a means of preparation for worship of the holy God. YHWH is taken to be completely holy, completely distinct; there is no one like YHWH, and so Israel in covenant relationship with this YHWH is to live in a holy or distinct way. Holiness is not a way of living in *separation from* the world but a way of *relating to* the world as a distinct people in relationship with the covenant God YHWH. A good example is the introduction and conclusion of Leviticus 18 (vv. 1–5, 24–30), which urges the community to live not as the Egyptians or Canaanites but as the people of YHWH. The community is called to live in the world as YHWH's people. The remainder of the chapter instructs in that context on matters of incest. The Holiness Code deals with life in both worship and ethics. Leviticus 23 delineates the calendar of festal worship with special feasts in spring (Passover and Unleavened Bread), summer (Weeks and Pentecost), and fall (New Year, Tabernacles, and Day of Atonement). The festivals are

8. A number of scholars suggest that the Priestly block of material including Leviticus has been edited by a Holiness School rather than seeing the refrain in Lev. 17–26 as evidence of a unified document.

central to this community's shared memories of Passover, of the giving of *torah* (at Pentecost), and of the wilderness experience in the Feast of Tabernacles. The patterns of harvest shared in the ancient Near East are also reflected in the festivals. Leviticus 24:1–9 attends to regular worship. Leviticus 25 provides an example of ethical implications of holiness, with rest for servants, animals, and the land in the Sabbath pattern and with its extension in the Year of Jubilee as an opportunity to make a fresh start in the face of debt and servitude.

Covenant and Creation Theologies in Numbers

Numbers gets its title from the numbering of the people as a beginning to the process of organizing them as a covenant people. Chapters 1–10 pursue the theme of the right ordering of life as people of YHWH. The texts operate on a very practical level. They do not theorize about principles for ordering life as this community of faith but rather give specific instruction in organizing the community to prepare to leave Sinai. These chapters function as covenant instruction and also reflect the theological perspective that the covenant God YHWH is also the creator who provides for the community's life together. These instructions often seem outdated and obscure to contemporary readers, but they have an embodied theological significance in ordering life as YHWH's covenant people with the defining divine presence at their center as they prepare to depart from Sinai.

Instructions for Maintaining the Centrality of the Divine Presence

The movable sanctuary, the tabernacle, is at the center of the camp, indicating the centrality of the presence of YHWH for the community. The tabernacle includes the most holy place with the ark of the covenant, the sanctuary, and then the sanctuary's courtyard, where sacrifices are offered. The priestly clan, which cares for the sanctuary, is the Levites, and they are deployed around the sanctuary at the center of the camp. The twelve tribes are organized around the Levites. The

Nazirites, who also embody ancient Israel's holiness, are specified in the organization (Num. 6). This order of the camp serves as instruction in embodying the reality that this community is centered in the divine presence. The ground-level organization suggests the community's identity as YHWH's covenant people. There is an order surrounding the central divine presence. Note that the Levites guard the sanctuary to protect YHWH's presence but that they also protect the tribes from the power of the divine presence. Should the community violate this divine presence, the consequences for the community could be drastic, as the narratives in Numbers demonstrate. The Levitical presence protects both the holy sanctuary and the people from potentially disastrous results when the people bring trouble by way of sin and uncleanness.

Instructions for Renewing Covenant Relationship

The community's departure from Sinai in Numbers 10 transitions to the book's second major theme—rebellions in the wilderness. The theme really begins in Exodus. Following the deliverance from the forces of Egypt at the sea, the people begin to complain that they have no food or water—as they had in Egypt. Their complaint leads to the provision of water, quail, and manna in various narratives. The theme is also clearly present with the rebellion of the golden calf, which we saw previously. These texts demonstrate the dialogical character of Israel's faith, the understanding that trouble and woe can disturb the divine-human relationship and that the covenant God can renew that relationship when it is fractured.

The numerous rebellions challenge the authority of the covenant God YHWH and of those YHWH has designated as leaders of the community. The consequence is wandering in the wilderness. Numbers 22–24 provides an interesting wilderness narrative with the lead character of Balaam, a wandering seer/judge/sage whom one of the surrounding kings hires to pronounce a curse on Israel. Such a curse was understood to be an effective weapon. In a complicated process,

YHWH sees to it that Balaam pronounces a blessing instead on Israel, showing that Israel will move to the promised land as a community with the covenant God and creator YHWH even in the face of various forms of opposition. The Balaam narratives provide comic relief amid the grim and at times bizarre passage through the troubles of the wilderness. The wilderness generation passes from the scene, and a new generation is numbered in a new census in Numbers 26 as the people prepare to move toward the land of the ancestral covenant promise.

Covenant and Creation Theologies in Deuteronomy

The Pentateuch concludes with the lengthy and influential book of Deuteronomy. Covenant forms its key theological dimension. It calls for covenant faithfulness in a new day and does so in a distinctive literary way. It proclaims *torah* as covenant instruction in a sermonic style that urges the community to live this *torah*. The significant confession of faith in 6:4–5 summarizes the theological setting of the book. "Hear, O Israel: The LORD is our God, the LORD alone. You shall love the LORD your God with all your heart, and with all your soul, and with all your might."

Deuteronomy bases the covenant in the mighty acts of YHWH in delivering ancient Israel from Egypt and exhorts the community to respond with covenant fidelity as they prepare to enter the land promised to them.

The God Who Delivers and Provides Torah for Human Response

The covenant instruction in Deuteronomy is based in God's mighty acts of deliverance from bondage in Egypt (4:34; 5:15; 7:19; 11:2–4; 26:8) and his continued presence. The language of the exodus tradition characterizes Deuteronomy's historical memory, and the divine presence is often portrayed in terms of the place where the divine name is present (12:5, 11, 21; 14:23–24; 16:2, 6, 11; 26:2). A name is more than an identifier here; it embodies the character of this God. To say that the divine name is present (in the sanctuary) is to say that YHWH is present, though not limited to that place. The understanding of covenant we have already encountered shapes the book's contents.

Following the historical account of Sinai and the wilderness wanderings, the book moves to the recounting of the covenant instruction central to the treatise. This recounting concludes with an exhortation to live this covenant *torah*. Chapters 27–28 lay out the consequences of keeping or breaking this covenant relationship for future generations. Deuteronomy 30:15–20 encapsulates the book's exhortation to decide "this day" for or against covenant fidelity. In the narrative framework of the Pentateuch, the exhortation is preparation for life in the land that stands before the community. The book of Deuteronomy is a central text in the covenant history and theology of the community of ancient Israel.

The God Who Blesses

While organized around the understanding of covenant, the book also uses the language of blessing, especially with reference to the land. Deuteronomy 7:12–14 makes clear that the fertility of land and of family constitutes blessing, not of the fertility gods of Canaan but of the creator. The framework of covenant loyalty includes divine blessing and calls for living in loyalty to the creator. Human response to divine creation fits both covenant and creation theologies. Worship in the sanctuary celebrates the gifts of blessing from the creator.

Concluding Thoughts on Covenant and Creation Theologies in Deuteronomy

Deuteronomy brings the Pentateuch to an exhortative conclusion, insisting that the covenant God YHWH brought Israel into a life-giving relationship through mighty acts of deliverance in the exodus from Egypt and that this covenant God insists that this people find wholeness of life in a faithful relationship with this God. Dabbling with "idols" brings only death, and so this community is called first to hearken to YHWH (6:4). The theological perspective of Deuteronomy insists on one God and, as a consequence, on one central sanctuary for the worship of that God. This YHWH is a jealous God—that is, a God zealous for ancient Israel to enjoy wholeness of life, found only in covenant fidelity with YHWH. The covenant relationship is initiated by the mighty acts of YHWH in the exodus from Egypt. The question in Deuteronomy is whether Israel will embody this relationship in all of life. Much depends on this decision, and much of the demonstration of this decision comes in Israel's ethical life, on which Deuteronomy gives extensive instruction. Deuteronomy is an extensive sermon on covenant fidelity in the context of the God who has delivered in the exodus. While covenant theology is the central organizing perspective, the book also understands the life on the horizon for the community in the land in terms of blessing and so partakes of that dimension of creation theology. The book frequently summarizes its theological perspective as an indication that it is not a legalistic checklist but a Mosaic perspective on the whole of life with the covenant God YHWH. The book is thus an appropriate conclusion to the Mosaic Torah. A characteristic example of such a summary is 27:9–10: "Then Moses and the levitical priests spoke to all Israel, saying: Keep silence and hear, O Israel! This very day you have become the people of the LORD your God. Therefore obey the LORD your God, observing his commandments and his statutes that I am commanding you today."

Conclusion

The starting place proposed for this account of Old Testament theology is the confessions of faith in the book of Psalms and their suggestions of creation, covenant, and prophetic theological perspectives. This provides a cogent organization of the plethora of theological perspectives in the Pentateuch.

Genesis begins with creation traditions in which God blesses with a divine presence that makes it possible for women and men to grow and thrive in the world provided for a whole life together. The creation traditions also make it clear that the divine hope of wise living for humans goes astray from the beginning of human history, but even so, the promise of divine blessing continues through the generations. That blessing takes a particular form of the promise of land and progeny to the ancestors, and in some ways, the central part of the story of ancient Israel sees the fulfillment and trials of that promise for the community. There are also covenant dimensions to Genesis texts, with both the Noahic and Abrahamic covenant traditions. The first half of Exodus comes explicitly to covenant theology with the divine deliverance of Israel from oppression in Egypt. The oppressed community laments, and YHWH hears and comes to deliver. The law codes that follow direct the community's response to this gift of liberation. The Priestly material, including additional instruction manuals, also reflects back to the creation theology in Genesis and makes it possible for the divine presence to tabernacle with ancient Israel. The holy covenant God can then journey with the community and provide the gift of wholeness for them. The journey for the community continues toward the promise, and the Pentateuch concludes with the majestic covenant sermon named Deuteronomy. With its emphasis on covenant fidelity and ethical traditions in the law codes as well as traditions of divine liberation of the oppressed community, Deuteronomy also suggests connections with prophetic theology.

This formative part of the story of God with ancient Israel portrays YHWH as the creator who provides fullness of life for the community and for all of creation. Vitality is tied to the divine presence tabernacling with the community. Covenant traditions characterize God as the one who hears and comes to deliver from trouble and woe, but the dialogue does not end there. This covenant God also offers the gift of direction in living as a people covenanted to God, the one who makes possible fullness of life. Living in *torah* embodies that fullness of life. The journey of the Pentateuch, even through the wilderness, brings ancient Israel to the edge of entering into the promise, a promise that continues to endure in the face of multiple twists and turns.

This story becomes part of the memory of the community, a memory that has persisted through many centuries and is part of the shared memory of today's community of faith. That memory of the God who is present to bless and who comes to deliver shapes the view of the current community that life centers on a relationship with this extravagantly generous God. This is the God who instructs in full living and who invites wise daily life. This God is the creator who keeps creating new possibilities for the human community. The memory of that God in these stories undergirds living with hope. Yet the blessing and the gift of life are not given only to enjoy but to share extravagantly and to shape the care of all creation. That is the shape of creation fidelity and covenant fidelity. Note that the broad genre of this text of the Pentateuch is narrative. The five books provide the foundational narrative for the faith community. The story provides a script for life, a purpose, as the community lives in relationship with YHWH, especially in relation to ethical issues and worship. The Pentateuch is an identity-forming narrative, a narrative of many dimensions, a narrative that places Israel among the community of peoples. This narrative of YHWH with ancient Israel constitutes the theology of the Older Testament.

In order to have a future, the narrative must continue, and the place provided for the care of the ongoing narrative is worship. Worship is central to the whole of the Pentateuch from the earliest altars, to the mobile tabernacle, to provision of sacrifice, to the march through the wilderness, to the central sanctuary of Deuteronomy. In worship the narrative of God with the community is remembered, reenacted, and experienced again so that it can shape life and faith. Here the community believes again the story and sees it shape all of life. Sigmund Mowinckel talks about religion in terms of worship, belief, and ethics.[9] Worship helps us comprehend belief and inspires ethical living. Belief gets demonstrated in living and brings the community back to worship. Ethical living enacts belief and inspires worship. It all begins with worship, and worship feeds the community's memory of its faith story so

9. Mowinckel, *Psalms in Israel's Worship*, 1:17.

that the community can encounter wholeness and embody and share it. It is in worship that the community's story, and the divine-human relationship, is re-membered, renewed, and enlivened. The worshiping community provides the means of shaping theology for living.

Some readers will be puzzled and disturbed at some of the narratives and legal traditions in the Pentateuch. There are troubling and difficult texts in this first part of the Bible. There are also troubling and difficult parts to life. As to the legal materials, they are never a legalistic checklist to earn divine favor. They are always in response to divine blessing and deliverance. They are also tied to the variety of lived experiences. The law codes in the Pentateuch are not static but dynamic and tied to daily life. These are not dusty, rigid, dead pronouncements of the past but are directions for living in relationship with the creator and deliverer, and these directions live in a cultural context. The narratives and legal codes in the Pentateuch both embrace and shape the culture from which they derived. They operate on the basis of the relationship with YHWH. They also reflect their originating culture and so are in profound ways different from contemporary narratives and law codes. Readers need to be committed to learning from such texts that disturb and confront. Readers also need to remember that the defining question is, What is God doing in this text? God is blessing and delivering and communicating with the community and with all of creation through the community. When that question is the focus of our theological attention, readers can begin to see the significance of even difficult narratives and legal codes. Theology is, after all, a word about God.

Finally, we should think further about the operative hermeneutic for reading Scripture. The hermeneutic followed in this volume is both literary and theological. It is essential to follow the plot or sequence of the text and to ask the question of the nature of the divine interaction with creation and the human community. The hermeneutic clearly includes the sociohistorical contexts from which the texts of Scripture emerge, because God was engaged with real life in the culture of that community. Yet the divine-human interaction is not limited to that originating historical context. It is also not limited to the questions that shape contemporary life. The texts stretch human response to them by broadening life contexts and questions. Texts give clues to interpretive communities. The revelatory language of these texts invites readers to join the story and shape memory and life narrative for contemporary readers. Perhaps poetry provides a model in calling readers to embrace and engage texts and encounter the mystery of revelatory texts. The Pentateuch showcases such engaging language from Genesis to Deuteronomy. A liturgical community can nurture and embrace such language.

4

Historical Books

T he next portion of the Protestant canon is the Historical Books of Joshua, Judges, 1–2 Samuel, and 1–2 Kings, as well as several books that relate to ancient Israel's time of exile and beyond, 1–2 Chronicles, Ezra, Nehemiah, Ruth, and Esther. Contemporary Protestant readers of the Older Testament will likely be familiar with this grouping of books. The Hebrew canon is organized somewhat differently. Its second portion is the Prophets, comprised of both Former Prophets (Joshua, Judges, 1–2 Samuel, and 1–2 Kings) and Latter Prophets. The language of the Former Prophets shows considerable influence from the language and thus the theology of Deuteronomy, with its emphasis on covenant. The central themes of the books focus on the relationship of YHWH with ancient Israel during their time in the land of Canaan from entrance to exile. Deuteronomy both concludes the Pentateuch and introduces the Former Prophets in terms of its language and theological perspective.

In addition to the Former Prophets, this chapter will also discuss books that relate to ancient Israel's time of exile and beyond, such as 1–2 Chronicles, Ezra, Nehemiah, Ruth, and Esther. Together with the Former Prophets, these are categorized as the Historical Books. The recounting of Israel's story in the Historical Books, covering

approximately six centuries, has a central theological dimension tied
to covenant, but it also has ties to creation and prophetic theology.
Therefore, this chapter will explore the contributions of these historical
texts to the creation, covenant, and prophetic theologies introduced in
the previous chapters.

Some basic orientation will aid readers. At the end of the Pentateuch,
the community of ancient Israel stands on the cusp of the land promised to the descendants of Abraham and Sarah. In the book of Joshua,
Israel emerges in the land of Canaan, and the next book recounts the
early experience of the community in the land during the time of the
judges. The books of Samuel portray the community's move to a monarchy and the time of the Davidic kingdom. The kingdom then divides,
and the story of the Northern and Southern Kingdoms comes in the
books of Kings. These conclude with the fall of Jerusalem. The books
of Chronicles give another account of the history of ancient Israel,
while Ezra and Nehemiah move beyond the sixth-century-BCE fall of
Judah. The books of Ruth and Esther also reflect this later period in
the history of ancient Israel.

Covenant Theology in the Former Prophets

The history in the Former Prophets is recounted from its end—that is,
from the perspective after the fall of Jerusalem in the sixth century.[1]

1. The composition, editing, and unity of the Former Prophets or the so-called Deuteronomistic History (DtrH) is still a complicated, highly debated subject. For the two most influential
theories in the history of the conversation, see Noth, *The Deuteronomistic History*; Cross,
Canaanite Myth and Hebrew Epic. Noth sees Joshua–Kings as markedly different literature
than that of the Pentateuch. He argues that Joshua–Kings is a unified work by one author (not
a redactor/editor, but an author)—the Deuteronomist (Dtr). He hypothesizes that the Deuteronomist had access to the Deuteronomic Law (the original book of Deuteronomy) and wrote an
introduction and conclusion to make the larger book of Deuteronomy as a sort of introduction
to the DtrH. According to Noth, the Deuteronomist worked around 562 BCE—so, during the
exilic period—in order to explain the loss of the kingdom. Within the DtrH, Noth identifies
the following characteristics that demonstrate a cohesive work: speeches by major figures at
key transitional points, specific language and vocabulary, one major theological stream, specific
chronology, and general style.

Cross, the founder of the "Harvard school" of thought, instead envisions a block model of
sources for the DtrH. Cross identifies two major editions of the DtrH, which he labels "Dtr1"

One of the defining questions in the history is why the Israelite monarchies came to end: What caused the fall of Israel and Judah? Based in Deuteronomy's perspectives, the historians recounting ancient Israel's experience make clear that covenant was central to this question. The fall of Jerusalem is tied to covenant breaking. The story in these books recalls again and again how the community broke covenant and renewed it by way of repentance. This community keeps breaking covenant until finally the community ends up in exile. Interestingly, the book of 2 Kings ends with the release of the Davidic king from prison in exile. Is there yet hope for the defeated community?

Covenant Theology in Joshua

Joshua is an account of Israel's emergence in the land of Canaan as a community delivered and shaped by YHWH and now in a place to embody the covenant life. The narration draws attention to Israel's status as the covenant community when the ark of the covenant leads them across the Jordan River, when all the males take the covenant identity marker of circumcision, and when all Israel celebrates the Passover. After the apportioning of the land to the tribes, the community gathers to renew their covenant relationship with YHWH and with one another in line with the covenant theology of Deuteronomy. True to that theology, the ceremony emphasizes the mighty acts of YHWH on behalf of this community and then calls for them all to "serve the Lord" in covenant faithfulness (24:14–15). The book of Joshua shows this covenant community learning to embody covenant life and practice covenant faithfulness in their surrounding culture once they enter the

---

and "Dtr2." Dtr1 was composed in the preexilic period, whereas Dtr2 was composed during the Babylonian exile. Dtr1 introduces two major themes: the sin of Jeroboam and God's faithfulness to the house of David. Davidic kings are portrayed as mostly good, particularly Josiah. Dtr1 functions as a message to the Northern Kingdom to return exclusively to worship of Yahweh at the Jerusalem temple. In addition, it serves as a message to the Southern Kingdom that restoration depends on the nation's return to covenant relationship with Yahweh. Dtr2, recording the fall of Jerusalem, reshapes history, blaming the fall of the Southern Kingdom on the wickedness of Manasseh. Dtr2 also emphasizes the message that Yahweh will not forget the covenant with their fathers and that there will be a return from captivity and restoration if only they will repent.

land of Canaan. The covenant God makes it possible to live in divine-human relationships in that setting, fully engaged in hard-won life.

Joshua 1–12 portrays the faithful covenant community emerging in the land. The covenant God YHWH, as noted in the covenant markers cited above, comes to confirm Joshua's leadership of the covenant community with the angelic theophany at the end of chapter 5 and to direct the plan of battle. Chapter 6 recounts the siege of Jericho. The ark of the covenant and priests and the processions around Jericho with trumpets and horns make clear the ritual nature of the siege. YHWH's covenant people take possession of the city. God has brought victory to them, from the planning of the siege—including the involvement of Rahab and the spies Joshua sent to reconnoiter the land—to the complete giving of the city to YHWH. Things change quickly in the next chapter. Viewing Joshua through the lens of covenant theology allows us to see Israel's first military defeat as a form of divine instruction. It reinforces for Israel the communal nature of the covenant and demonstrates the consequences of covenant breaking. Following the battle of Jericho, Israel is surprised to face defeat at Ai. Achan, among the Israelites, kept some of the rewards of the victory. These battles are understood to be battles of YHWH, and so the rewards are to go to YHWH. Achan has brought defeat on Israel. He, his family, and his possessions are destroyed. Eventually Ai is defeated, but this account shows that there are consequences to breaking covenant. It also shows the corporate dimensions of covenant life. Achan was connected with his family and possessions, and they all suffer as a result. Israel also suffers for the actions of this one. The life of faith in the Former Prophets is not primarily individualistic. Rather, the covenant relationship is between YHWH and the community. The community is foremost, and Achan's misstep harms the community.

The second half of Joshua recounts the distribution of the land among the tribes. With the covenant community in the land, the Deuteronomic promises have come to pass (Josh. 21:43–45). The book concludes with a covenant ceremony for this generation now in the land. It summarizes the mighty acts of the covenant God YHWH on behalf of the ancient community and seeks the people's response to this covenant revelation in worshiping only YHWH (Deut. 5:7; Josh. 24:16). The ceremony then renews the covenant between God and people. Wholeness of life is encountered in the blessing of covenant faithfulness. Many readers will likely be familiar with the scholarly tradition of interpreting covenant texts in the Older Testament in the tradition of Hittite treaty formulas. Covenant peoples encounter blessing as they keep the treaty relationship's instructions. The book of Joshua portrays this reality of covenant blessing and cursing in Israel's emergence in the land.

The Book of Judges

If the first half of Joshua pictures obedient Israel possessing the land, Judges pictures disobedient Israel struggling in the land. The Deuteronomic hope of keeping covenant suffers in Judges. The book recounts the stories of six major judges (Othniel, Ehud, Deborah, Gideon, Jephthah, and Samson) alongside minor judges by way of what is labeled the Judges cycle, introduced in Judges 2. Israel does evil in the sight of God and suffers oppression as a consequence. The people cry out to God, who raises up a judge to deliver them. The way back to hope for this covenant community is the cry to the covenant God YHWH. God has not forsaken them, even in their so-called dark ages, but hears the cry of repentance and comes to deliver by way of judges. The stories are told vividly and at times with dark humor, such as in the story of Ehud. The stories do not, however, simply repeat the Judges cycle. A downward spiral becomes evident in the life of the community in this tribal confederation. The two stories that conclude the book illustrate in stunning ways the idolatry, conflict, and inhumanity to others that came to characterize this early time of Israel in the land. The picture is of covenant faithlessness and its consequences.

A particularly gruesome example comes in Judges 19–21. A conflict arises between a Levite and a wife. She is not named, and the term signifying her is often translated as "concubine," but the conflict seems to be over the tradition of the marriage. Will it be lived out in the Levite's residence (patrilineal) or in the residence of the wife and her family (matrilineal)? The story is told with considerable narrative skill and detail. A simplified summary would indicate that the wife journeys to her family's residence, and the Levite goes to take her back to his residence. On the trip, they stop for the night in Gibeah in territory belonging to the tribe of Benjamin. Finally a man offers them hospitality—as was the expectation—for the night in his residence. In the course of the night, a crowd of ruffians shows up seeking the Levite so that they "may have intercourse with him" (19:22). The host offers his daughter and the Levite's wife in place of the Levite. The crowd refuses, but the Levite gives his wife to them. She is assaulted and raped. In the morning, when the Levite is set to leave, he finds his wife lying at the threshold of the house (dead or nearly dead?). He places her on a donkey and continues the journey. At his home, he gruesomely dismembers the wife into pieces and sends the pieces to the tribes to call them to gather against the tribe of Benjamin for this outrageous and scandalous crime. The leaders declare war on the men of Benjamin, who are eventually defeated. Then the leaders realize they must have a way for the tribe of Benjamin to find a future. They capture the town of Jabesh-gilead, whose men had not participated in the *herem*, war of destruction, against Benjamin, and take their women for the Benjamite men. They also then kidnap women from Shiloh to complete the task. This account of the narrative is very brief and simple and probably downplays the shocking rape, pillage, and abuse that characterize the plot! What is such a narrative doing in the Bible, and what are readers to do with it when considering the theological import of this story?

These questions are difficult and this volume will not do justice to them, but I hope to show how understanding the text through the interpretive framework of covenant theology helps makes some sense of it.[2] Before we discuss the theology, though, note that such a nar-

---

2. See Bergmann, Murray, and Rea, *Divine Evil?*; Römer, *Dark God*; Seibert, *Disturbing Divine Behavior*; Seibert, *Violence of Scripture*.

rative as Judges 19–21 is in the text. The Hebrew canon is true to life and painfully honest. This kind of narrative dramatizes the worst of human behavior; there is no denial of it here. It must be admitted in order to deal with it as a community. The theological perspectives of the Older Testament seek to address the whole of human life, even the horrendous parts. The sexual assault and abuse against women in these texts horrifies, and, what is more, such behavior continues in the twenty-first century! Such behavior murders the equality the divine creator established between men and women created in the image of God. An honest reading of the text scandalizes.

That said, we come to the theological dimension that is the primary purpose of this volume. The most important element in interpreting any text in the Bible is the matter of context. The context in Judges 19–21 makes clear that the inhospitable, vile, and abusively violent behavior against other humans and often against women demonstrates how existence in this covenant community has come to the absolute bottom of what could even be considered human. Judges traces a downward spiral in which the community's patterns have reached the depths of scandal and covenant faithlessness. This behavior is despicable and is there to horrify readers. The theology is Deuteronomic. YHWH delivered the community of ancient Israel so that they could live together in wholeness, but they have completely corrupted the covenant instruction so that chaos and death are at hand. The corruption of covenant instruction under the judges highlights an important plot in the Former Prophets, which is clearly articulated in the concluding verse of Judges: "In those days there was no king in Israel; all the people did what was right in their own eyes" (21:25). Thus, Judges serves in part as a polemic in favor of a monarchy for ancient Israel. The tribal confederation of the judges was a failure on several fronts. At the same time, the Former Prophets indicate that no political structure will solve the community's issues. Monarchy is also at best a necessary evil. The most basic question is the question of Deuteronomy: Will ancient Israel keep covenant with YHWH, who has created this community?

Creation, Covenant, and Prophetic Theologies in Samuel and Kings

The narrative of the united and divided kingdoms recounts the major transition in ancient Israel to monarchy and the story of Israel's covenant keeping and covenant breaking in this period. These texts are central in the story of YHWH's relationship with ancient Israel. Both Mosaic and Davidic expressions of covenant are part of the story. The Former Prophets interpret the experience of monarchy in theological terms. Creation, covenant, and prophetic theologies shape the narratives. Royal texts picture YHWH as the deity who is present to bless the Davidic line and enable it to thrive and mediate blessing to the people. The editorial frame of these books leans on the Sinaitic covenant traditions as determining the life of the community and so interprets this era in terms of fidelity to these covenant structures.

It becomes clear in these books that the prophets (e.g., Samuel, Nathan, and Elijah) are central interpreters of and advocates for the covenant in Israel. By way of the prophets, YHWH speaks to the people by addressing the king and calls for faithful response to divine revelation, often in the language of the call for repentance. These texts view Israel's experiment with monarchy from the perspective of the exilic community. The metanarrative views the Davidic dynasty as a gift from the creator akin to the ancestral promise to Abraham and Sarah. The creator is present to bless the community so that it thrives and is able to share blessing with other peoples. David, Solomon, and Josiah, for example, have a lasting influence that encourages wise living. In the end, however, the prophetic warnings from Samuel and Nathan and other prophetic figures, to the effect that kings are inclined to lead the people astray and away from covenant fidelity, come to difficult fruition. The kingdoms fall along with the hopes of Jerusalem, and the texts confirm the warnings about and even judgment on the corruption and injustice and idolatry of the community led by these kings. That seems to be the dominant theological perspective of the Former Prophets. This look at these historical books confirms the dialogue and creative tension between creation and covenant theologies in these texts. The community's responses of wisdom and covenant fidelity fall short, as prophetic figures articulate in the text.

Movement toward a Monarchy

Folly, covenant breaking, and injustice all come to the fore in these narratives, calling for repentance and a return to a faithful divine-human encounter. The books of Samuel also bring together a variety of materials: traditions related to Samuel, the ark of the covenant, the rise and fall of Saul, the rise of David, and the court history of David. All of the traditions in this literary setting are focused on the question of the community's response to the covenant God YHWH. The Samuel narratives picture the community, in the tradition of Judges, as living in a time of corruption and inattention to the covenant with YHWH. The prophetic perspective of God's speaking by way of the prophet and calling for repentance serves this theological frame. Especially in the Davidic narratives, matters of creation and wisdom also become part of the picture. All the texts work from a theological frame of divine revelation and human response. Often that response is tied to the covenant perspective. The narratives serve as instruction in living as the covenant community and so further the Deuteronomic exhortation to fullness of life in relation with the covenant God.

Viewing the narratives of Samuel and Kings through the lens of covenant theology results in numerous theological insights. First, it connects the people's request for a king with their lack of understanding for how to live as the covenant community and be faithful to the covenant instruction. The early chapters of Samuel recount events tied to the ark of the covenant as the chief symbol of the divine presence with Israel, especially events surrounding a disastrous conflict with the Philistines at Aphek-Ebenezer (1 Sam. 4–6). The account is laced with pointed humor when the Philistines capture the ark and its presence does considerable harm to their idol Dagon. The ark is returned to Israel's territory, but the narrative suggests that the community of ancient Israel does not even know how to serve the covenant God YHWH in a faithful way. This theological confusion leads the community to the request for a king.

First Samuel 8–9 furthers this connection between their inability to exercise covenant faithfulness and the request for a king. Chapters 8–9 are central texts for the theological understanding of kingship in ancient Israel. The time for a loose tribal confederacy has come to an end for this community. The Philistines press them on many fronts, and given the geography and the lack of a central organizing authority, the Israelites find it difficult to communicate. The people around them seem to be progressing with monarchies, and so the representatives of the people ask their leader Samuel for a king. Samuel warns the people of the dangers involved. A king could lead the people away from their covenant relationship with YHWH and toward the idols and rulers of the surrounding peoples. The peoples around the Israelites and their worship of the Baals brought the real threat of syncretism, the mixing of religions. However, the Israelites disregard this danger to covenant faithfulness and press Samuel for a king. The community does not see how essential covenant is for their life together; they do not know how to live as a covenant community.

The framework of covenant theology also helps illuminate the role of Israel's king. In their history, ancient Israel had encountered royal figures in Egypt who were understood to have divine characteristics. Israel's tradition reacted against such a view, because the covenant God YHWH is understood to be Israel's only God. The theological conclusion of this debate over monarchy comes to the establishment of a ruler who serves as YHWH's representative in ruling over the people of the covenant. The king will also represent the people in their relationship with the covenant Lord. So Israel accepts a human king who is a kind of intermediary enjoying a special relationship with YHWH: to the people he represents YHWH as ruler, and before YHWH he represents the people. This sort of regime is often called sacral kingship. To judge from the narratives, this theological solution is something of an uneasy compromise. Both supportive and suspicious attitudes toward monarchy come forward in the Former Prophets. The prophetic view of ancient Israel's history, aligned with the view of Deuteronomy (17:14–20), casts doubt on the wisdom of moving to a monarchy as the reality is played out in the stories of the united and divided kingdoms. Up to the rise of David as king, the narratives of the Historical Books appear to stand solidly in the stream of covenant theology: the community of ancient Israel has entered into covenant by way of divine deliverance from Egypt and is called to respond by way of covenant instruction such as that in Deuteronomy. The question is whether this community can summon fidelity to this covenant relationship. The royal texts that follow in Samuel and Kings have something of a different theological perspective as they now interweave aspects of creation and covenant theologies.

The United Monarchy

The united monarchy, which lasted nearly a century, includes the reigns of Saul, David, and Solomon. All three reigns demonstrate the interplay between creation theology and covenant theology in numerous ways. First, we see God acting in these royal texts from behind the scenes. The action takes place in the days of the royal family in public and private contexts. YHWH is the one who is present, undergirding the promise to David and his family. God makes it possible for the dynasty to grow and thrive in the world. Royal texts in the Older Testament are often undergirded by such a creation theology perspective. God is the one who brings order and is present to bless.

At the same time, the second theological implication comes from the context in the Former Prophets and particularly in its view of the direction of ancient Israel's experience with a monarchy. The overarching editorial direction of the books of Samuel and Kings is at best cautious about monarchy and its power. This Deuteronomic theological viewpoint does not center on the success or popularity of the ruler but on the community's covenant faithfulness in the relationship with YHWH. Saul as the first king is in some ways portrayed as a judge and is popularly acclaimed as king, but the transition to David is difficult.

In 1 Samuel 13, Saul's covenant breaking comes to the fore, and his inability to lead the covenant people begins to emerge. Chapter 15 portrays Saul as covenant breaker and his tragic decline begins to dominate the narrative. Covenant theology makes a place for human rulers but insists that they live in faithfulness to covenant *torah*. Even Nathan's prophecy in 2 Samuel 7 makes this point about the faithfulness of Davidic rulers. This text is often taken to be the first articulation of the Davidic covenant, which is often contrasted with the Mosaic covenant because the Davidic covenant emphasizes promise rather than the response shaped by *torah*. And so texts in the Deuteronomic framework suggest that the community's allegiance to the Davidic tradition leads to a diminution of covenant faithfulness to YHWH shaped by the Sinai tradition. At the same time, especially the Bathsheba episode portrays the prophet Nathan as a covenant spokesperson for YHWH calling the king to repentance and covenant faithfulness, and the king immediately repents and finds a way through to hope in everyday creation theology. The interplay of creation and covenant theologies is instructive for interpreters.

Solomon's reign more than Saul's or David's showcases creation theology. He did well with economics and administration, and wisdom and culture thrived during his time as king. An important text in the Solomon story is 1 Kings 3, where YHWH asked what Solomon needed to rule and Solomon asked for wisdom. In that chapter, Solomon is characterized as one who embodies wisdom. The Older Testament continues this connection between Solomon and wisdom. That suggests that these royal texts are also undergirded by creation theology, in which God makes it possible for this king to discern wisdom and live by it. The positive side of Solomonic kingship is this wisdom and culture, in which YHWH is present to make success and growth possible for the kingdom. The downside of Solomonic rule, however, reflects the concerns about monarchy found in Deuteronomic covenant theology. Influenced by foreign alliances, Solomon becomes an oppressive ruler who dilutes the covenant fidelity of ancient Israel. The Deuteronomic theologians are suspicious of creation/wisdom theology. Will it lead this community astray from its essential identity as YHWH's covenant community? That is the editorial frame of the Former Prophets.

The Divided Kingdoms

Following the death of Solomon, conflict leads to a division of the kingdom into the Northern Kingdom (Israel) and the Southern Kingdom (Judah). The remainder of Kings recounts the narrative of the divided kingdoms by telling the stories of the various kings in Israel and Judah. The two standard measures of that faith are fidelity to the pure worship of YHWH in the Jerusalem temple and fidelity to the covenant with YHWH. The kings of Israel never meet that standard. It is the prophets who advocate for covenant loyalty. Echoes of Deuteronomy 17:14–20 run through these accounts. In a sense the two standards of faithfulness represent creation theology (temple) and covenant theology (fidelity). These theological perspectives shape the narratives. The temple is replete with creation imagery and reminds the community of the creator. The worship there is a human response to the revelation of the creator. The kings edge the community toward covenant disobedience and so toward wrong response to revelation of the divine one who delivers and initiates a covenant community. This theological perspective is reflected in one of the organizing markers of the texts. The accounts of the kings of the divided kingdom begin and end with standard introductions and conclusions for each king. These help keep readers on track in the narrative but also provide the opportunity to comment on the faithfulness or faithlessness of the king. Often the king "did what was evil in the sight of the LORD," as had those before him. Some kings "did what was right in the sight of the LORD"; the criterion for the evaluation is Deuteronomic: Did the king remain faithful to covenant with YHWH with an emphasis on true worship of YHWH in the Jerusalem temple? Covenant theology and creation theology are central to the organization of the commentary on ancient Israel's monarchy, as was prophetic theology in this tradition. How the kings as representatives of the community responded to

YHWH's revelation was central to the community's hopes, a tradition often associated with David.

From the perspective of covenant theology, the Northern Kingdom is disastrous. The kings lead the people away from responding to YHWH's covenant instruction with loyalty. For example, pure worship of YHWH in the Jerusalem temple, which is the test of covenant loyalty, ceases when Jeroboam I establishes worship centers at Bethel in the south and Dan in the north so that travelers support the economy of their own kingdom. This move also keeps worshipers away from the Davidic theology established in Jerusalem and encountered on pilgrimage to festivals there. Golden calves are set up at Bethel and Dan and further lead the people away from covenant loyalty to YHWH. This lack of fidelity to the covenant prompts the emergence of prophetic theology interacting with covenant theology and calling for faithfulness and just living. When a reader puts these various perspectives together, then the judgment that the Northern Kingdom is guilty of heresy also interweaves creation and covenant theologies. The sanctuaries suggest wrong creation theology and wrong worship of the gods and goddesses. The human relationships suggest injustice and covenant disobedience. The prophets speak in the name of the covenant God and creator YHWH to call the people to turn to true worship and justice.

Prophetic theology emerges as YHWH uses prophets to speak on behalf of the divine one, calling the people to respond with fidelity to their creator and liberator. The interaction between covenant theology and prophetic theology is on full display in the Elijah and Elisha narratives. For example, the abandonment of covenant fidelity under the influence of Queen Jezebel results in syncretism with Canaanite fertility religions. The dramatic encounter in 1 Kings 18 between Elijah and the prophets of Baal exemplifies the conflict, as does the story of the illicit royal annexation of Naboth's vineyard (1 Kings 21). Corrupt royal power and the influence of idolatry are at the center of this story of the consequences of infidelity to the covenant with YHWH. Elijah and Elisha become the advocates for covenant fidelity, even to the point of Elisha's support for the overthrow of the Omride dynasty. Eventually the Northern Kingdom falls to the Assyrians. It had been a kingdom with little stability; kings often lasted a very short time. The books of Kings proclaim the reason: they broke covenant with YHWH.

The Southern Kingdom experiences greater stability; its royal figures continue primarily in the Davidic tradition. The major concern of the textual tradition is whether these kings keep covenant. That would determine Judah's future. Prophets such as Isaiah advocated for faith in YHWH as the way forward, but the proclamation of prophetic theology often landed on deaf ears, whether of people or of kings. The story does not often celebrate the royal figures. One exception is King Josiah. He led the people in a covenant renewal that brought hope and reform in Jerusalem (2 Kings 22–23). A scroll of the Torah guided this reform and is often associated with Deuteronomy. It emphasized covenant faithfulness and obedience to *torah* as well as faithful worship of YHWH in the Jerusalem temple. The dominant direction of Jerusalem's monarchs, however, was not toward obedience to the creator, deliverer, and guide who was Judah's God but toward breaking covenant, and so by the end of Kings, Jerusalem and Judah go the way of defeat and exile.

Covenant and Creation Theologies in 1–2 Chronicles, Ezra, Nehemiah, Esther, and Ruth

An additional account of the history of ancient Israel comes in 1–2 Chronicles, Ezra, and Nehemiah. The books come from Jerusalem after the return from exile and contribute to our understanding of that setting and its context. The books take up the historical accounts in the Former Prophets as well as other records and memoirs in order to shape historical accounts relevant to this new context and from distinct viewpoints. The short stories of Esther and Ruth also come from this time period and each has distinct emphases related to divine providence. Despite being composed later than the other Historical

Books, all the books from this period continue to embrace creation, covenant, and prophetic theologies and include both divine revelation and human response in their theological articulations. Chronicles, Ezra, Nehemiah, Esther, and Ruth all appear in the third and latest section of the Hebrew Bible, the Writings. While articulations vary with genre and setting, the theological perspectives noted from our exploration of the Psalms persist.

In Chronicles, for example, covenant theology is at the heart of the narrative, and creation theology runs through the genealogies and the emphases on royal ideologies and cultic matters. The Chronicler writes to articulate an identity for the Second Temple Jewish community, an identity based in history and providing hope for a new context and for the future. Restoration and covenant renewal are at the heart of these historical texts. These texts suggest strongly that YHWH continues to be present with the Second Temple community to make possible for them a full life of blessing. The covenant identity of the community shapes their view of the world and their distinct identity in it. The struggles in Second Temple Yehud (that is, the remnant of Judah under Persian rule) characterize life under threat, and part of the response is the encouragement of Chronicles as well as the clear definition of the community so that it will survive for the future.

Ezra and Nehemiah also reflect this same era. Ezra has a priestly tone and focuses on the reestablishment of the temple. Chapter 9 also indicates that prayer has moved toward the confession of sin and so is tied to the theological perspectives of both covenant renewal and repentance. Governor Nehemiah's prayer explicitly speaks to the "God who keeps covenant and steadfast love with those who love him and keep his commandments" (Neh. 1:5). The reading of the Torah and the renewal of covenant as the context for Torah are central to the community's identity in Ezra and Nehemiah in this Second Temple period.

Covenant theology also appears in Esther, but the articulation is unique in its Second Temple context. Esther reflects a strong emphasis on divine provision for this community as part of the Persian Empire. Queen Esther leads the people to resist those who would oppress the Jewish community. In line with Chronicles, Esther tends toward a particularist or exclusive view of the community. The concern is that the community survive opposition and pressures toward assimilation by way of nurturing their particular identity through such a short story. The theological perspective that God will particularly preserve the Jewish community leads to an emphasis on the distinctive characteristics of this people as God's people. The trauma of defeat and exile brings a variety of responses in Yehud. Certainly one of the important responses is an emphasis on the distinctiveness and identity of the community as it seeks to come to terms with life as part of the Persian Empire. This view is a particular articulation of covenant theology present in the Second Temple period.

Ruth is similar in its emphasis on divine providence, but the major theological perspective comes from creation theology rather than covenant theology. This short story emphasizes divine providence, but the providence is hidden and comes to fruition in the relationships of the story. Ruth and Naomi face life-threatening crises but show loyalty in their relationships, as does Boaz, who helps make survival a reality. This account tends toward a more universal or inclusive view. God is the God of all people, even of a Moabite woman (Ruth). In the realities of the Persian Empire, the Jewish community needs to relate to all people. The Moabite Ruth is even part of the royal Davidic line. This story reflects the creation theology emphasis on the divine blessing that the community is to share with all peoples. The book of Jonah seems to take a similar view; we will attend to that in the chapter on the Prophets. Ruth and Jonah are in tension with Esther, but all of these short stories are significant in the Second Temple period. They seek to address how the Jewish community is to live as part of the Persian Empire: Should they emphasize their Jewish identity or embrace the reality that all peoples are created by YHWH? These short stories suggest some of the issues facing the Jewish community in the Second Temple period.

Conclusion

The narratives of this chapter operate from and intertwine creation and covenant theologies and include prophetic theology; tensions between the various perspectives come to the surface. The Historical Books come to the end of the Davidic kingdom, a traumatic end of defeat and exile. The hope of justice in a Davidic kingdom crumbled, and the temple/priestly hope for atonement literally came to ruin. The place and hopes for persons, families, and the community came to a bad end at the hand of the Assyrians and the Babylonians. These historical texts raise many questions. Why did the fall of Jerusalem in the sixth century come to pass? Where was YHWH? What about the future for the remaining remnant of Judah? Chaos has come to rule the day. These questions of theodicy vex ancient Israel as part of the shape of this most powerful community trauma in the life of Israel. The center of life has not held; life as they have known it for centuries has disintegrated into chaotic ruin. Where is the creator who is present to bless? Where is the liberator who hears and comes to deliver? Where is the God who speaks in dialogue with the people of Israel? What is to come of Israel and Israel's faith? In the coming chapters, these narratives begin to take poetic form as striking expressions of these searing questions of faith. It is in liturgical communities that these sets of shared memory are best preserved as a foundation for current communities of faith, also living in a world characterized by chaos on every side.

5

Psalms

Chapter 2 of this book argues for a shape for Old Testament theology that begins with the Psalms as the community's confession of faith. The poetry of the Psalms takes the form of prayer and praise and so is tied to the central act of worship in faith. These poems are organized in a particular way in the Hebrew Psalter. The opening poem contrasts the righteous and wicked and encourages the righteous to follow divine instruction for living, suggesting that the psalms to follow are now part of that divine instruction. Psalm 2 then introduces the Davidic king as the one chosen by YHWH to rule. The king faces enemies, and that leads to a number of psalms that relate to the conflicts of life. Most of the psalms in book 1 (Pss. 1–41) are prayers for help (laments) from individuals in trouble and woe. Book 2 (Pss. 42–72) continues with a predominance of individual laments from the context of trouble and woe. Concern with enemies pervades a number of these prayers. Interpreters have noted the contrast between the righteous who offer the prayers and the enemies who oppose both the righteous and YHWH. The speakers seek divine help, refuge in YHWH. Book 3 (Pss. 73–89) carries more of a community emphasis and relates to the fall of Jerusalem in the sixth century BCE (Pss. 74; 79; 89). The experience of defeat and its relationship to the God who delivers and blesses comes to the fore. The Davidic kingdom established at the beginning of the Psalter (Ps. 2) is no more.

A number of interpreters see books 4 and 5 as responding to the dire straits and searching questions at the end of book 3. Book 4 (Pss. 90–106) begins with a psalm of Moses to take the community back to a time before there was a kingdom of David; it then moves quickly to a celebration of the reign of YHWH (Pss. 93–100). The praise of YHWH as creator and ruler calls the community to sing a new song even in the midst of the defeat of the Davidic kingdom and its center in Jerusalem and the temple there. Community psalms of praise are more prevalent in the latter parts of the Psalter. Book 5 (Pss. 107–50) continues to relate to the experience of defeat and exile and its aftermath, as indicated in its opening psalm. A central text in this last portion of the Psalter is the lengthy acrostic on divine instruction (Ps. 119). It is followed by the Psalms of Ascent (Pss. 120–34). This collection remembers pilgrimage to Zion and the community's yearning for the divine presence there. With additional lament psalms, the Psalter moves to its fivefold conclusion of emphatic praise. The Psalter has moved from its opening poem emphasizing keeping *torah* through the honest dialogue of faith to the joyful praise of YHWH, who is present to bless. In one sense, the entire Psalter is responding to the divine revelation. In another sense, the perspectives of creation, covenant, and prophetic theologies, central to this volume, derive from the Psalms. The divine-human encounter permeates the Psalter.

Recent decades have witnessed few studies of the characterization of God in the Psalms. Robert L. Foster provides an exception. His first sentence is "This is a book about God."[1] My approach to the Psalms and theology is a variation of his, and so it may be helpful to consider his work. Foster notes things that have distracted scholars from a focus on the character of God in the Psalter: the nature of Hebrew poetry, the relation of the Psalms to Christianity, and the gripping portrayal of human experience in the Psalms. Foster seeks to explore the portrayal

---

1. Foster, *We Have Heard, O Lord*, 1.

of God in the Psalms and does so by attending to the Psalms in sequence according to the five books of the Psalter. He surveys the various psalms in order with an emphasis on divine action and characteristics.

In book 1 God is primarily gardener and divine King who hears lament and rescues. Book 2 brings a good bit of variety in the prayers to the God of Zion though articulating hope in God's steadfast love and motherly compassion. Book 3 is characterized by the alternation between trouble and hope in terms of theological conflict. The book ends with a passionate petition for help articulated by the community. Book 4 invites the singing of a new song to the divine King while also articulating the need for the King to save the current generation. The lengthy concluding book of the Psalter moves toward praise of King YHWH.

Foster concludes the volume with a chapter on the imitation of God, emphasizing the teaching of the Psalter in terms of godly virtues and how readers might learn those. He often labels the persona of the poetry of the Psalms as preacher or prophet; at other times he suggests that the words of the psalm are the words of the congregation of ancient Israel. His emphasis on ethics is noticeable, and his emphasis on the importance of proclaiming the Psalms laudable.

My variation on Foster's approach is to emphasize the question of what YHWH is doing in the text. I combine that focus with the assertion that the canonical shape of the Psalter turns its prayer (that is, plea, lament) and praise—a human address to God—simultaneously into divine instruction to the community of faith. The didactic function of the Psalter is thus at the fore in creation, covenant, and prophetic emphases. This is particularly noticeable in terms of prayer and praise in the Psalter, which will be the primary focus in this chapter.[2] The laments in the Psalms bear witness to a genuine covenant interaction. Many of the hymns of praise reflect the creator who rules over all of creation. Royal and wisdom psalms also contribute to that perspective. In a number of psalms God also speaks about worship and fidelity to

---

2. For more on this view of the Psalms, see Bellinger, *Psalms as a Grammar for Faith*.

the relationship with YHWH, an emphasis of prophetic theology. The three theological perspectives permeate the Psalms.

A Covenant Theology of Prayer

The dominant genres in the Psalter are plea and praise. Of those two, plea dominates the opening portions of the book, and so it is appropriate for a theological reflection on these psalm genres to begin with plea. That also fits the experience of many people of faith as they begin in the very depths of human experience. There are more individual lament psalms (pleas) than psalms of any other genre in the Hebrew Psalter. One of the influential introductions to the Psalms in the twentieth century was Bernhard Anderson's *Out of the Depths: The Psalms Speak for Us Today*. The preposition in the subtitle is important. Anderson agrees that the Psalms speak to us but also presses the understanding that the Psalms speak *for* us. That is, in the Psalms the saints of old pray, and we can pray as they prayed. One of the significant theological perspectives in reading and interpreting the Psalms is the sense that they teach us to pray. I take these texts to constitute a school of prayer. Such a practice of reading and praying requires readers and petitioners to become steeped in the language of address to God, and in time one sees the contemporaneity of these ancient texts as well as their remarkable authenticity. The lament psalms teach readers how to pray as the texts articulate in gripping ways the language of trouble and woe. Indeed, the most striking thing about these psalms of lament is their honest dialogue of faith. This language of prayer is not idealistic but realistic, not cliché but honest—at times, brutally so.

In these psalms, the ancient community of faith is making sense of experience—one definition of theology. We have seen that in covenant theology in the Older Testament, the rehearsed faith tradition is that YHWH is the covenant God who hears and who comes to deliver. In these prayers, the speaker or the congregation is not encountering deliverance and is therefore crying out for an audience with the covenant God. These texts are genuine covenant interactions between God and the worshiping community. I take the theological significance of these texts to be quite remarkable. In most covenant theology in the Hebrew Bible, the call is for the community to follow covenant instruction and live out *torah*—that is, God's covenant requirements for faithful living. In these texts, we find the other side of the covenant dialogue of faith, the call for God to act as the covenant God who hears and comes to deliver. In this other side of the covenant dialogue of faith, ancient Israel holds YHWH accountable for the history and faith the community has learned, and so the prayer is above all transparent. Deuteronomy 6 calls for Israel to "hear"—that is, keep covenant. The lament psalms call for YHWH to "hear"—that is, keep covenant.

The context of the Psalter is important at this point. The introductory poem gathers the participants in what is to follow in the book— God, the righteous who pray, and the enemies who oppose both God and the righteous. The psalm begins with a beatitude for the righteous, those who do not follow the ways of the unjust but who follow and are immersed in the ways of the righteous, embodied in the *torah* of YHWH, covenant instruction that directs faithful living. This opening wisdom of the Psalter suggests that what follows in the book also now becomes part of the divine instruction for living faithfully. And what follows is instruction in a central dimension of that life, prayer. I have labeled the Psalms as a grammar of faith, and instruction in prayer is central to that grammar. With this introductory psalm, the Psalms as human prayers addressed to YHWH have become also God's Word addressed to humans as instruction in prayer.[3] In the Psalter, people of faith learn how to pray.

The lament psalms are bold acts of faith from individuals and from the community in the face of trouble. These texts can be rather jarring from the perspective of contemporary Western culture and its tendency to deny death and pain. The Psalms are transparent and engage in a process in which the way to hope is through fear, the way to joy through trouble, and the way to peace through hostility. Denial of these harsh

---

3. Childs, *Introduction to the Old Testament as Scripture*, 513.

realities does not constitute faith but rather leads to nurturing grudges and fear. Speaking boldly to the covenant God YHWH is the path of faith, calling on God to embrace pain and placing trust in this God. The cry is not only venting frustration but is addressed to the covenant God, who has demonstrated the listening ear and the move to liberate. And the covenant God YHWH accepts these utterly honest prayers. This community never moves beyond addressing God. The name Israel ("struggle") suggests those who strive with God, and that is what happens in these prayers, an honest covenant interaction. These model prayers are bold and liberating and frightening. They frighten because they call petitioners to trust this covenant God with what will happen. The prayers address YHWH as the covenant God known in the community's tradition and so are explicitly theological as part of the I-Thou relationship. Psalm 42, a lament and the opening psalm of book 2, highlights this understanding. The divine presence is as vital to life for humans as is water for the doe. The community has learned of this covenant God by way of its historical narrative when God created this community for justice and faith in the deliverance from Egypt; the lament psalms persist in that faith with passion. The faith in the God of persistent love and trustworthiness is bold and does not relent; it is a candid faith in the covenant God, who does not leave the community alone but hears and comes to deliver. The urging in prayer is that God will not relent but will stay with this community of worship, justice, and faith. Such a covenant theology of prayer requires the ongoing practice of candid prayer and trust.

Viewing the lament psalms through the lens of covenant theology brings considerable depth to the theological shape of the Psalms and of the Older Testament. Contemporary readers may come to the honest dialogue of faith in individual prayer and come to see the brutally honest language of these prayers as the language of deep and trusting relationship. The prayers are passionate and honest. When readers understand that, comfort with the language is possible. The petitioner needs to see the language as personal and realistic rather than artificially prescribed. It may well seem excessive to contemporary readers and petitioners, but this intimate language marks the covenant relationship with YHWH. Such powerful language to articulate pain is central to the process of moving to hope and renewed life when life is in the midst of turmoil. These prayers are intimate and personal, but they are also public and relational prayers; they are part of the liturgy of covenant faith.[4] When such language is absent from the congregational prayer, there is no model for growth in the relationship with God, and absence of struggle in that relationship leads to stagnation in faith and confirmation of the status quo. These texts provide the opportunity to call YHWH to transform life. The intimate and troubling language of these prayers is central to encounters with the covenant God at the deepest level.

Laments are cries to YHWH in the midst of trouble. These texts address YHWH, portray the crisis at hand, and plead for help in passionate ways. These prayers often come to a hopeful conclusion. An important dimension of these texts is that they show considerable boldness in the covenant relationship with YHWH. In the global sense, YHWH initiates the covenant relationship that creates Israel as a community. That reality befits the pattern of revelation and response, but inside that life-giving relationship, all the way through the long history of lament in the Older Testament, Israel takes initiative in these prayers and in furthering the relationship in this crisis. The lament psalms are genuine divine-human interactions in the covenant relationship with YHWH. The theological perspective of the petitioners is classic covenant theology in ancient Israel's tradition. The historical psalms recount that theology based in the mighty acts of God. God is the liberator who hears and comes to deliver, but that is not happening in this crisis, and so, in the honest dialogue of covenant faith, petitioners—whether individuals or the community—complain to God that God is not fulfilling the expected task of deliverance. The covenant community is processing its experience in that relationship and calls on YHWH to bring about the expected deliverance. In the lament psalms, the degree of urgency and passion in the petition varies. In some cases,

4. See Brueggemann, "Costly Loss of Lament."

the petition comes in an attitude of trust; in others the petition is a full-blown complaint spoken with considerable bluntness. The honest dialogue of covenant faith is on full display; clearly, the primary lesson in the Psalter's school of prayer is complete candor in the relationship with the covenant God. Lament is the dominant voice in the book of Psalms. That voice includes penitential psalms (e.g., Ps. 51), though those texts are a minority voice. Plea psalms enrich the narrative of ancient Israel's covenant theology and demonstrate how it converses with the community's ongoing life and how it can be remembered and renewed in liturgy.

Imprecatory psalms are particularly troubling for readers of faith, sometimes called prayers for vengeance. Probably the parade example is Psalm 109. It is a covenant prayer, petitioning God to come and deliver, and so instructs in a covenant dialogue of faith, a divine-human encounter. The context from the petitioner is that enemies have mercilessly attacked the speaker with words of hate. And so the petitioner addresses the covenant God of justice in petition:

> May his days be few;
>   may another seize his position.
> May his children be orphans,
>   and his wife a widow.
> May his children wander about and beg;
>   may they be driven out of the ruins they inhabit.
> May the creditor seize all that he has;
>   may strangers plunder the fruits of his toil.
> May there be no one to do him a kindness,
>   nor anyone to pity his orphaned children. (vv. 8–12)

The plea is for complete divine vengeance to fall upon this enemy, with the punishment fitting the crime, a familiar call in contemporary language. Such a prayer is an embarrassment to many faithful readers of the Psalms. If you look at the NRSV rendering, you will see that the words "They say" have been added to the beginning of verse 6 to suggest that this prayer recounts the words of the enemies. Some argue that the Hebrew grammar supports such an addition, but there is no textual basis for it. The best reading is that this petition comes from the petitioner, who has been wronged. Interpreters must see that this prayer is addressed to the covenant God YHWH, the one who can transform the harsh reality that has occasioned the prayer. The one who has been wronged could either strike out in violence, or deny the need for vengeance and allow a grudge to fester, or fervently plead with the God of justice for deliverance.

The most familiar imprecatory psalm is a powerful expression of grief over the fall of Jerusalem in the sixth century. The grief expressed in the opening lines of Psalm 137 often brings empathetic response from readers/hearers, but the conclusion of the psalm shockingly articulates beatitudes for those who will bring recompense upon the enemy Babylon and its allies with the violent destruction of any future for their military might by way of the killing of their babies. The psalm's socio-historical background of horrifying defeat helps readers to understand these hopes of powerless exiles. The poem becomes a powerful act of faith with the public claiming of pain and screaming it to the covenant God of justice. As I indicated, the enemies are one dimension of the portrayal of crisis in the lament psalms, characterized broadly as a sojourn in Sheol, the realm of the dead. The power of death has invaded life and gripped the person or community, diminishing life in some way. Sheol is portrayed elsewhere as a deadly place of no return, a place without community and a place beyond the presence of God. What is remarkable about these psalms is that the lamenters continue, in this traumatic experience, to address the covenant God and commonly come to a hard-won hope. They move through the deathly experience toward a new view of life; they come to a renewed sense of covenant with the God who hears and who comes to deliver.

The Praise of God in the Psalms

The two dominant psalm genres are plea and praise. We have seen that the pleas or lament psalms primarily function with a covenant theology in which YHWH is portrayed as the God who hears the cry and comes to deliver. The psalms of praise also operate at times with such a covenant perspective, especially in what are often called psalms of thanksgiving. Also relevant are the historical psalms of praise that recount the salvation history of ancient Israel, how God has through mighty acts and faithful humans and various other ways delivered the faith community of ancient Israel. These declarative psalms of praise are related to the broader, descriptive psalms of praise, which portray God as creator, liberator, and teacher. It becomes clear that the three perspectives of creation, covenant, and prophetic theologies are all connected to the psalms of praise. These texts are vibrant and varied and express in joyful wonder and awe great enthusiasm for God. They often follow a basic pattern: a call to praise, followed by a reason or reasons for praise, and concluding with a renewed call to praise similar to the introduction of the poem. The body of the psalm, containing the reason for praise, often articulates divine actions or attributes by way of Hebrew participles, relative clauses, divine epithets, or passages initiated with the Hebrew particle *ki*, meaning "because" or "for." And so the bodies of various psalms of praise articulate important theological material in the Psalter. Some psalms of praise focus on covenant theology, some on creation theology, and some interweave the two perspectives.

Thanksgiving psalms typically come from the perspective of covenant theology, and Psalm 30 is a prime example of this. The first five verses articulate the purpose of giving praise and thanks to YHWH and invite the congregation to join this narrative memory as a means of entering the experience that encourages faith. The psalm then narrates the testimony of this witness to the covenant God, who hears and comes to deliver. Verses 6–7 narrate the crisis leading to the plea in verses 8–10:

> To you, O LORD, I cried,
>> and to the LORD I made supplication:

. . . .

> Hear, O LORD, and be gracious to me!
> O LORD, be my helper!

The persuasive petition leads to the account of deliverance in beautiful poetic imagery:

> You have turned my mourning into dancing;
> You have taken off my sackcloth
> and clothed me with joy. (v. 11)

The psalm concludes with a renewed vow of thanksgiving to the God who delivers. The body of the psalm bears witness to a genuine pastoral transaction of deliverance by the covenant-making and covenant-keeping YHWH. This psalm declares the narrative of crisis and divine help for the one giving thanks and provides a clear and beautiful example of covenant theology in a psalm of praise.

The extraordinarily brief Psalm 117 illustrates well how psalms of praise often interweave creation theology with covenant theology. The psalm begins with "Praise YHWH," a hallmark of the descriptive psalms of praise. It is a call to praise, and thus not praise itself. The drama of the psalm is how the community will respond to this call.

> Praise the LORD, all you nations!
>   Extol him, all you peoples!
> For great is his steadfast love toward us,
>   and the faithfulness of the LORD endures forever.
> Praise the LORD!

Note that the call to praise is universal and that the reason for praise is tied to special vocabulary in the Psalms, the divine *hesed* and *'emet*, persistent love and trustworthiness. The community of ancient Israel has learned from the narrating of its history that God's powerful kindness and fidelity stand in the midst of many life experiences. This language seems to echo the covenant history of the exodus, but the call to worship is universal. The divine engagement with the human community is not limited to the heirs of Abraham and Sarah but includes all nations and thus relates also to the character of the creator, who continues to be present and give life to humans. Divine engagement with ancient Israel also suggests that divine engagement with all of creation and all of the nations is not far away. This text thus suggests both covenant and creation theologies. Divine constancy and fidelity call for fervent praise of YHWH.

A number of the descriptive psalms of praise operate from a base of creation theology. An important example is the collection of psalms in book 4 that celebrate the reign of YHWH (Pss. 93–100). Psalm 96 provides a prime example, beginning with an extended universal call to praise, opening with the first verse:

> O sing to the LORD a new song;
>   sing to the LORD, all the earth.

The psalm suggests that the reign of YHWH happens "today" in worship, calling for a new song and hope in divine justice and righteousness. The realities of ancient Israel's life do not always match this hope, but the new song embraces hope. Ancient Israel is called to sing to YHWH as the creator who is present and active in the community.

> For all the gods of the peoples are idols,
>   but the LORD made the heavens.
> Honor and majesty are before him;
>   strength and beauty are in his sanctuary. (vv. 5–6)

Remarkably, then, all of creation is called to sing a new song of praise to the creator, who will bring justice and righteousness for all of creation. Such power of persistent love and fidelity is possible with the glory (presence and activity) of YHWH. This celebration of the divine presence of the one who blesses in creation confirms again the centrality of the temple as a place of divine presence (Pss. 46; 48). The sanctuary is known to be the source of life (46:4), bringing refuge and hope in the midst of whatever life brings. YHWH is the one present in Zion to provide the nourishment for full living. The reality of divine presence to bless the community is enacted in worship in the sanctuary. Psalm 48:9 suggests that YHWH's persistent love is dramatized or enacted in worship.

> We ponder your steadfast love, O God,
>   in the midst of your temple.

The translation "ponder" is a wholly inappropriate translation of the verb; it means "to act out or represent." The community again encounters the divine ruler, the creator who brings hope and order to the world. So Mount Zion and its environs are to be glad, for the creator of persistent love and fidelity and blessing is present to give life.

These descriptive psalms of praise indicate that the means of praising God is to remember and narrate the story of God's presence, activity, and communication to bless, liberate, and guide. God's people must do so honestly and in uninhibited and substantive ways. The praise of God in the Psalms weds candid and powerful emotion and reason. A reason is always articulated for praising God. Both praise and lament in the Psalms are essential. The God of the Psalter is present to bless and comes to deliver. Such a confession of faith in the midst of the trouble and woe ancient Israel encountered prompts profound and important conversation about theodicy, a central theme of the Psalms. Psalms of praise that celebrate the reign of YHWH in the latter part of the Psalter speak that theme into a context of the aftermath of defeat and exile. The two themes must then interact. At times the result is a song of protest.

Prophetic Theology in the Psalms

The hymns of praise include the voice of prophetic theology. Psalms 15 and 24 are examples of instructions related to entrance into worship. Both texts strongly affirm the connection between worship and the rest of life, a theme important in the Latter Prophets. All of life belongs to the creator. Both of these psalms articulate important instruction in the preparation for worship in ethical rather than ritual terms, also consonant with the emphases of the Latter Prophets:

> O Lord, who may abide in your tent?
> Who may dwell on your holy hill?
>
> Those who walk blamelessly, and do what is right,
> and speak the truth from their heart. (15:1–2)

> Who shall ascend the hill of the Lord?
> And who shall stand in his holy place?
> Those who have clean hands and pure hearts,
> who do not lift up their souls to what is false,
> and do not swear deceitfully. (24:3–4)

The second note of prophetic theology comes in psalms of praise that also include direct divine speech. Psalms 50, 81, 82, and 95 include prophetic oracles. Each of these poems bases its theological perspective in the praise of God and then quotes God, who speaks of the shape of the life of faith. Psalm 50 envisions a theophany in which God speaks first to Israel (vv. 7–15), calling for a life of faithfulness to the creator of life and to the creator of the covenant community.

> Call on me in the day of trouble;
> I will deliver you, and you shall glorify me. (v. 15)

God then addresses the wicked (vv. 16–23) with a call to righteous living. Psalm 81 begins with praise to the God who, beginning in verse 5 (with v. 5 introducing the address), addresses the people with a call to faithful living. Psalm 82 is unusual in that God here addresses even the divine council, urging support for justice.

> Give justice to the weak and the orphan;
> maintain the right of the lowly and the destitute.

Rescue the weak and the needy;
    deliver them from the hand of the wicked. (vv. 3–4)

Psalm 95 begins with praise of the creator and covenant-making God and concludes with a call to the community for faithful living.

These divine oracles include several accounts of the historical memory of ancient Israel's faith traditions and combine both creation and covenant emphases. While they do not dominate the book of Psalms, these prophetic texts do find a voice in the Psalter. If we envision these psalms in ancient Israel's public worship, perhaps it is appropriate to see these texts as part of the faith in which those called as prophets were immersed. The Psalms are about the divine-human encounter, beginning with divine revelation and moving to human response. Perspectives of creation, covenant, and prophetic theologies move through these worship poems.

Royal and Wisdom Perspectives

The dominant voices in the Psalms are those of plea and praise, noted above. Scholars rightly add to these the distinctive voices of both royal psalms and psalms with wisdom themes. Royal texts are tied to events in the lives of Davidic kings—coronations, battles, and a psalm on the occasion of a royal wedding.

In several of these texts, the language of the Davidic covenant is important. Psalm 2 speaks of the Davidic line of kings as a gift of the creator chosen to reign in Jerusalem as YHWH's representatives. The king's gift and blessing for the community is justice, a central dimension of a complete life for YHWH's people. Laments and expressions of thanksgiving are also included in these royal psalms, especially tied to defeat, victory, and prayer for the king in battle. We have already noted the connection to the Davidic promise in Psalm 89. Psalm 45 celebrates a royal wedding with an emphasis on divine blessing for the royal couple. God has chosen the Davidic king to represent YHWH in ruling over the people in Jerusalem and to represent the community in addressing YHWH. The king is important in the dialogue of faith between YHWH and Israel. The creator who reigns grants this gift of leaders as part of the divine blessing on the community.

Another gift from the creator is wisdom. Wisdom teachers learn the orderly processes of life as God created it and then pass on this wisdom to the community of faith. These wisdom texts often contrast the wise and foolish or the just and unjust as a means of encouraging wise living. Therein is found the divine blessing of a life of integrity and learning. It is the good life and the morally good life. A variety of voices come to the fore in these wisdom texts, as we will see in the next chapter on wisdom theology. At times, the initial impression of a simple moral calculus sounds like a theology of health and wealth (Pss. 37; 133). At other times, questions about the prosperity of the wicked and issues of theodicy become pressing (Pss. 49; 73; 112; 127; 128). The approach to these issues varies considerably in these texts. Psalm 73, for example, raises profound questions about prosperity and poverty and their relationship to faith. Psalms 2, 19, and 119 celebrate *torah* as a gift of instruction in wise living. Psalm 78 understands history also as a gift for learning to live wisely. Undergirding these texts is the theological perspective that God created life and the world and placed wisdom in the creation. Such wisdom as these psalms bequeath becomes a blessing of the creator and a path for a life of integrity and wholeness. The next chapter will discuss further this language of wisdom.

Conclusion

This meditation on the Psalms and theology makes clear that both creation theology and covenant theology are present in major ways in the book of Psalms. The psalms of praise give broad voice to creation theology.

> The heavens are telling the glory of God;
>   and the firmament proclaims his handiwork. (19:1)

Psalm 8 celebrates the creation and the place of humans in it. Psalm 104 is a powerful meditation on God as creator and sustainer, the one who makes fullness of life possible.

> O LORD, how manifold are your works!
>   In wisdom you have made them all;
>   the earth is full of your creatures. (104:24)

> Let them praise the name of the LORD,
>   for he commanded and they were created. (148:5)

> The earth is the LORD's and all that is in it,
>   the world, and those who live in it. (24:1)

All the world belongs to God the creator. The portrayal of God in the Psalms gives full voice to creation theology. This creator rules and sustains life that embraces the hope of thriving and growing in the world. The Psalter also includes voices of wisdom as instruction in living on that kind of hopeful path as well as texts that articulate the gift of royal leadership.

Covenant theology also finds a major voice in the Psalter. The historical psalms of praise narrate the mighty acts of God in which God delivers and brings into being the covenant community, with *torah* as its hallmark. Exodus memories are important in these historical poems. It is also the lament psalms that take up a major portion of the landscape in covenant theology articulated in the Psalter. The laments are petitions in the midst of trouble and woe. They cry to the covenant God to liberate the individual or community from the bonds of death. These genuine pastoral interactions live as a significant embodiment of covenant theology in the Older Testament. The community takes much initiative in the divine-human relationship in these texts. The faith tradition has revealed YHWH to be the covenant God who liberates, and the petitioners in these texts insist that YHWH act in that way and deliver. The Psalter also makes space for a voice of prophetic theology in instructing the community to embody faith in all aspects of life. The distinctive in these texts is the revelation of the God who speaks and calls for a response of faithful living (repentance).

The theological dimensions of the Psalms are not controlled by one voice. The perspective is communal and relational. The perspective is about the dialogue of faith in a vibrant community life. Covenant and creation both are present and interact. Texts that begin with the history of the mighty acts of God to deliver and create a covenant community will include praise of God as creator. The same is true of lament psalms; they plead for the covenant God to deliver, and they also confess this God as creator and sustainer of life and humanity. Texts that begin with the praise of God as creator will also praise God as the creator with a history of delivering from bondage and even as creator of the divinely chosen Davidic king. Creation psalms celebrate the gift of *torah*. The interaction is not a contradiction; rather, there is a creative tension here. Neither perspective is primary. Both are present and contribute to the dialogue of faith in the Psalms. The tension is between a liberation theology with covenant instruction and a theology of presence with its gift of wisdom teaching.

6

Wisdom

The third section of the Hebrew canon is a mixed group of books and so carries the title "Writings." Psalms, Wisdom literature, and historical books are all included in this section, generally the latest of the three sections of the Hebrew canon. All of the books involved focus in one way or another on covenant and/or creation theology. We have already considered the Psalms in chapter 5 and Chronicles, Ezra, Nehemiah, Esther, and Ruth in chapter 4. This chapter will attend to the remaining books in the Writings, which come from the wisdom traditions and are based in creation theology. They demonstrate how the creator placed wisdom in the world and makes it possible for the sages to learn it and pass it on so that living in line with the created order is possible. It is a means of encountering blessing.

Traditionally, ancient Israel's Wisdom literature is designated as the books of Proverbs, Job, and Ecclesiastes. Proverbs teaches practical wisdom for living, and Job and Ecclesiastes question simplistic understandings of that wisdom around issues of undeserved suffering and the ordering of life. We will also include a brief look at Song of Songs and Lamentations as they connect to wisdom. The chapter will conclude with a brief look at Daniel, also part of the Writings in the Hebrew canon. This is included in the wisdom traditions because

Daniel narrates living wisely in exile in the context of an apocalyptic hope for the completion of the reign of God.

Wisdom

The Hebrew term for "wisdom" carries a variety of connotations in the various contexts in which it occurs. In summary form, the concept of wisdom in the Hebrew Bible includes the following:

1. Wisdom comes from experience or observation. Reflection on the events of daily living are central—events such as eating or speaking or laughing.
2. Wisdom is tied to morality and justice. It is about developing the good, moral life in major events, in the everyday, and in relationships. Social ethics in one's way of life are important to wisdom.
3. God is the source of wisdom.
4. Wisdom instructs in the life of faith, in a way analogous to the function of *torah*.

Wisdom consists in the relationship between God and humanity wherein humans seek to understand and live by the orderly processes of life. Recall that the theological underpinnings of wisdom are found in creation theology. In the other sections of the canon we have explored (Pentateuch, Historical Books, and Psalms), both covenant theology and creation theology, and prophetic theology as well, have been present in a variety of ways. The theological base of wisdom is essentially devoid of either a covenant or a prophetic emphasis.

The theological perspective in wisdom is creation theology. To articulate it again briefly, God creates the world and humanity and places wisdom in the world. God enables sages to encounter this wisdom and to pass it on in the teacher-student relationship. Students can learn wisdom and live by it. In so doing, they come to encounter fullness of life. That is part of the creator's blessing, the power to grow and thrive in the world. It will be clear from these last sentences that this creation theology is about the relationship of the divine with the creation and all who are in it. Theological reflections on the wisdom texts rooted in this creation theology will take a variety of forms, but the theological heart of the matter will be in God's creation. This theological background suggests that wisdom is universal, and that perspective is reflected in the interaction between ancient Israel's wisdom texts and those from surrounding cultures. The Egyptian text the Wisdom of Amenemope is often compared with Proverbs 22:17–24:22, and it is likely that the Proverbs text has a literary relationship with the Egyptian text. Several ancient Near Eastern texts related to theodicy are often also compared to Job. Wisdom is not limited to the experience of ancient Israel.

Creation Theology in Proverbs

Proverbs is a collection of sayings and so derives from various times and came to be associated with education in ancient Israel. The primary audience is likely young persons. The educational purpose of the book is clear in its opening poem, with the goal for the young to learn and live fully. The opening chapters set the theological base of wisdom in Proverbs and clearly tie wisdom to creation theology. YHWH creates wisdom, places it in the creation, and enables humans to find it. The gift of wisdom is the blessing of the creator, a means of growing and thriving in the world given by God. This is clearly seen in the following excerpt from chapter 3:

> The Lord by wisdom founded the earth;
>   by understanding he established the heavens;
> by his knowledge the deeps broke open,
>   and the clouds drop down the dew.
>
> My child, do not let these escape from your sight:
>   keep sound wisdom and prudence,
> and they will be life for your soul
>   and adornment for your neck. (3:19–22)

Embodying wise living is the appropriate response to the revelation of the creator. In the opening chapters, the revelation of wisdom is communicated in Woman Wisdom's call.

There has been considerable discussion about the background of Woman Wisdom in these chapters. Woman Wisdom in these texts is extraordinarily close to both YHWH and the creation. What seems clear in the text is that Woman Wisdom is a personification that makes it possible for YHWH the creator to speak in the first person and call to wisdom those who do not yet know it. The contrast between the wise and foolish ways of life are front and center in these texts. Those following wisdom will live while those following folly will die. The first chapter pictures Woman Wisdom as crying out in the streets to call the young to learn. The consequences for those who do not come to wisdom are dire indeed. The contrast to Woman Wisdom is Dame Folly, who seductively leads to death. The characterization of Dame Folly suggests connections to idolatry.

Chapter 8 is particularly important for seeing the connection between wisdom and creation. Chapter 8 begins with Woman Wisdom's call to learn, and the text again connects wisdom with reverence for God ("fear of the LORD"). The significance and power of Wisdom are central to this text.

> The LORD created me [Wisdom] at the beginning of his work,
>   the first of his acts of long ago. (8:22)

Creation comes about by way of Wisdom.

> When he [YHWH] assigned to the sea its limit,
>   so that the waters might not transgress his command,
> when he marked out the foundations of the earth,
>   then I was beside him, like a master worker;
> and I was daily his delight,
>   rejoicing before him always,
> rejoicing in his inhabited world
>   and delighting in the human race. (8:29–31)

This poem's articulating of the centrality of Woman Wisdom in creation leads to the notable call to wisdom concluding chapter 8.

> And now, my children, listen to me:
>> happy are those who keep my ways.
> Hear instruction and be wise,
>> and do not neglect it.
> Happy is the one who listens to me,
>> watching daily at my gates,
>> waiting beside my doors.
> For whoever finds me finds life
>> and obtains favor from the LORD;
> but those who miss me injure themselves;
>> all who hate me love death. (8:32–36)

After the call to wisdom in Proverbs 1–9, the book shifts to instruction in practical wisdom using a variety of proverbial sayings. At times, the sayings use basic comparisons, and at times they use similarities to make a point about life (16:8; 26:11). Sometimes the comparative element moves toward paradox, sometimes toward contrast (17:22; 27:14). Basic observations about life and the consequences of behavior from those characterized as wise or foolish teach the ways of life and their results (10:18; 16:18). The proverbial sayings are both brief and concrete as well as rhetorically appealing and relevant to the everyday. The sayings are traditional broad instructions about living fully and so articulate a moral order for living. They do not intend to instruct on all the questions of life. Rather, they are more along the line of warning signs that specify the tendencies or basics of life. The purpose of bequeathing this practical wisdom is to encourage readers/hearers to reflect on living in line with the created order. Such a human response to the revelation of the creator furthers theological encounter with the divine. One way to characterize these sayings is as observations for successful living, as ordered by the creator. This characterization can be seen in the following examples:

A false balance is an abomination to the LORD,
  but an accurate weight is his delight. (11:1)

The wise are cautious and turn away from evil,
  but the fool throws off restraint and is careless. (14:16)

Better to meet a she-bear robbed of its cubs
  than to confront a fool immersed in folly. (17:12)

Contrasts between the wise and foolish are clear and are reflected in the parallel structures of the sayings. Parallelism is one of the organizing principles for the sayings in Proverbs. The theological base of the sayings is in the order of creation and learning and living in line with that order. Therein is the encounter of divine blessing. Often the sayings take the form of traditional folk sayings without any explicit theological language, but the context in Proverbs ties the wisdom to the creator.

Longer sayings sometimes appear in the latter part of the book, such as Proverbs 27:23–27. This text describes a common agricultural scene of the day with flocks and grazing. In the pragmatic wisdom context in Proverbs, the flocks are understood as God's provision for life, and the text calls for wise use of the resource. The creator blesses with the materials of life and urges wise living in enjoying and using the materials to build a life of integrity in community. The text is a classic example of revelation and response in terms of practical wisdom based in creation theology.

The collections of proverbial material in Proverbs 30–31 are somewhat enigmatic. They seem to raise questions about the traditional sayings in the book. The book's concluding acrostic poem portraying the woman who embodies wisdom reminds readers of Woman Wisdom in Proverbs 1–9 and the divine call to learn and live fully in line with creation's order. Undergirding such a call to a wise way of life is the divine blessing characteristic of creation theology in the Older Testament.

Job

The theological reflection on Old Testament Wisdom literature in this chapter takes the pragmatic wisdom of Proverbs rooted in creation theology as a base and then moves to the texts that are more speculative in nature. They ask questions and examine closely an oversimplified version of the creation theology characterizing most of the proverbial sayings we have noted above. It appears that over time, orthodox wisdom in ancient Israel came to be seen as a rigid kind of vending machine theology in which each righteous or wicked deed put in the machine issued in a reward or punishment according to the nature of the deed. Such a rigid understanding of the order of life given by the creator does not stand up to the deep questions of life in the books of speculative wisdom. The first example, Job, is both remarkable and puzzling. What are we to make of it, and what is its contribution to wisdom theology and the broader theology of the Older Testament?

The book from its beginning deals with the undeserved suffering of Job, who is introduced as a "blameless and upright" man "who feared God and turned away from evil" (1:1). The problem is that the book does not give a satisfying solution to that issue. Elihu suggests a disciplinary view of Job's suffering, but that does not seem to fit the character Job or the book's perspective. This issue of undeserved suffering is often labeled with the term "theodicy," the vindication of the justice of God. The traditional formulation of the issue is how anyone can claim that there is an all-good and all-powerful God in the face of the evil and suffering in the world. Theodicy is a central issue in contemporary theological discourse, but this discourse can become very theoretical. Such theoretical matters are not central to Job. What is central in the text is the trouble in Job's life. The contrary example of Job's undeserved suffering contradicts a universal and rigid doctrine of reward and retribution and an explanation of the order of life based on righteous and evil behavior. Some have suggested that the key to understanding the theology of the book is the question put by the *satan* ("adversary") in 1:9: "Does Job fear God for nothing?" Is it possible for people of faith to serve God out of disinterested righteousness rather than for any benefits they might receive? A literary approach to the book suggests an interpretive focus on the speeches of YHWH in the culminating chapters 38–41. Might the book center in an encounter with the divine in the midst of trouble and woe rather than in theoretical explanations of suffering?

Many have attempted to interpret Job and have included issues such as theodicy, undeserved suffering, disinterested righteousness, the moral order of life, and encounter with the divine in the middle of suffering. All of these issues contribute to the book's significance. It is, however, the base in creation theology that ensures the book's contribution to Old Testament theology. Perhaps the shape of the book could provide a clue for interpreters. The prose prologue and epilogue frame a wisdom dialogue between Eliphaz, Bildad, and Zophar—advocates for popular traditional wisdom who explain the order of life in terms of rewards coming to the righteous and retribution coming to the wicked—and Job, who uses his undeserved suffering to question this orthodox wisdom. That structural view of the book along with the canonical strategy of interpreting the book in the context of the wisdom movement suggests the overarching theme of the limits of human wisdom. The conclusion of the book suggests that life has a moral order. The wisdom dialogue, the hymn to wisdom in chapter 28, and the divine speeches suggest that for humanity, many questions will never be completely answered. To put this view in another way, Job serves as a critical corrective to an overly simplistic interpretation of Proverbs as having settled the questions of the order of life and its ambiguities. The book is about the questions and wonders of life humans cannot explain. That is a considerable contribution to contemporary theology and life. The tie between Job and the wonders of creation as divine gift makes possible this crucial reflection on the limits of human wisdom.

A number of interpreters have noted connections between Job and the laments in the Psalter. Just as the petitioners in the lament psalms raise questions and protests in ancient Israel's covenant theology, so Job raises questions and protests in the community's creation theology.

Job's intense cries to God are prayers. There is a tradition of the patience of Job, based on a verse in the New Testament book of James (5:11). The translation there of the "patience of Job" is more properly rendered as the "endurance/persistence of Job." The character Job in this wisdom dialogue is not patient but is certainly persistent. In line with the lamenters in the Psalms, Job takes much initiative in raising profound questions in his opening lament in chapter 3 and does so by way of the language of creation. The traditional theology of creation of the day has come undone. The hymn to wisdom in chapter 28 and especially the speeches of YHWH in chapters 38–41 operate in the language of creation, and that language runs through the book. Job intensely proclaims that the creator's blessing is neither controllable nor explainable in human terms. It is YHWH who creates and rules and grants blessing and cursing, as the prose prologue suggests. Human growing and thriving in the world always comes to creatures from the creator. A wise life in response to the creator's blessing includes a large measure of understanding that humans will not always have the answers to the questions and troubles of life.

Ecclesiastes

In the reflection of Ecclesiastes, God is clearly the creator and the giver of life; the book suggests a wise, considered, and wondering response. It raises questions about traditional responses and understands these questions to be an essential part of the pilgrimage of faith.

The traditional connection with Solomon likely serves to lend the book the authority of wisdom, since the book at times deviates from traditional views. Early on, the treatise speaks of a series of experiments to determine the meaning of life, but no meaning is found. While wisdom is preferable to folly, even wisdom does not solve the pressing questions of life. Repeated themes throughout the book suggest this emphasis. For example, the first half of the book uses as a refrain "vanity and a chasing after wind" (1:14; 2:11, 17, 26; 4:4, 16; 6:9), and the second half often returns to the conclusion that humans do not know

A Framework for Reading the Wisdom Books

I. Proverbs

A. Reverence for God underlies all maxims, even if not explicitly stated.

B. The proverbs are understood as part of the instruction for honoring God and finding life.

C. No premium is placed on failure, indolence, stupidity, mediocrity, tactlessness, and friendlessness. The wisdom teachers value the opposite.

D. Wisdom is not automatic but needs to be learned. Proverbs are thus often pithy condensations of years of experience.

E. Wisdom celebrates life. Wisdom speaks little of disease, suffering, or problems. It may seem simplistic (in Proverbs), but wisdom gives guidance that represents tendencies.

II. Job and Ecclesiastes complement Proverbs

A. Job is partly a reaction against a simplistic understanding of Proverbs. It is concerned with how persons will or should react if all they value is removed. How can life be worthwhile when that happens?

B. Job protests against the wisdom of the day that claims humans can control life. If life has any inner reason, it is known to God alone. The character Job is not the model of the patient sufferer, the stoic. His is a mighty rage. Job asks angry questions and waits for an answer. God responds, "None of your business!" Life is in God's hands, not ours, so we are to put our faith in God.

C. Ecclesiastes asserts that life has order but that the control of that order does not lie with humans. Rather, glimpses of order are seen in the seasons and rhythms whose inner workings humanity cannot know.

Source: Adapted from Arterbury, Bellinger, and Dodson, *Engaging the Christian Scriptures*, 128.

the future (6:12; 8:17; 10:14). The concluding chapters of the book suggest that while humans do not know what is to come, the option for living in the present is reverence for God the creator of life and for God's instruction. The conclusion is clearly a wisdom hallmark. Divine ordering of life is the creator's revelation; human response centers on the realization that the creator freely gives life as a gift and does not always show how life will reveal its wonders.

The book's opening poem announces the theme of "vanity" in a variety of ways. The concept is important in wisdom reflecting on the wonder of creation. The word suggests brevity and futility. Readers would do well to remember that Ecclesiastes is a book about wisdom when articulating the significance of this poem. Qoheleth (the Hebrew transliteration of the term used for the writer of the book, best translated as "the teacher") appears to be concerned not so much about skepticism toward all of life as about skepticism concerning the human ability to control and arrange life. The teacher's experience defies a strict doctrine of reward and retribution that accounts for all the events of life. In the teacher's observation, what is true to life is the freedom of God. God is the one who gives life and reigns over life. Under this broad theme of the freedom of God, Qoheleth commends helping one another and making the most of the life God gives. Qoheleth is also of the view that being overly righteous and overly foolish are both death-giving (7:15–18).

Ecclesiastes is clever and surprises readers often with unexpected questions about life, faith, and wisdom. It takes the view that life has a rhyme and rhythm but that humans are not in a position to control the seasons of life such as love, joy, and death; God is the one who gives life. It is a book that requires wonderment and puzzlement from readers and interpreters. It is important to understand the book in the context of ancient Israel's wisdom tradition. It is not so much a work of nihilism as it is a rejection of the view that the community and its wisdom have explained all the questions of life and of theology. God is the one who creates and blesses and calls for wise responses. Responses of wonder, humility, and reflection deepen the sense of wisdom in this part of the Hebrew canon.

Lamentations

Lamentations grieves over the sixth-century destruction of Jerusalem and the temple. It is a series of acrostic poems lamenting the fall of the city and the devastation from it. The poems are analogous to the laments of the Psalter and are also often compared to other laments from the ancient Near East that relate to the destruction of cities. The poetry profoundly speaks deep grief and is an important part of the community's memory of this devastating event in their shared narrative. These poems also then teach grief and prayer in the midst of trouble and woe in the context of the covenant relationship. This didactic function has a wisdom dimension. Such a wisdom dimension is present with the five brief scrolls of the Megilloth (Ruth, Esther, Ecclesiastes, Lamentations, and Song of Songs) in the Hebrew canon. Each of them teaches in some way and so relates to the wisdom tradition.

Song of Songs

The association of the Song of Songs with the patron of the wisdom movement in ancient Israel, Solomon, connects the book with wisdom. There is a long tradition of interpreting the poetry allegorically in terms of God's love for Israel or Christ's love for the church, but the initial sense of the poetry in the ancient world is clearly about enjoying the basic wonders of life as God created it, including love between a woman and a man.

Song of Songs is based in a wisdom perspective tied to the creator and seeking a wise response to life as handed to characters and the community. The poetry is in a sense pragmatic wisdom for fully enjoying the life God has given humans in the creation, part of which is human love. Creation imagery permeates the Song. The woman and the man are pictured in creation imagery from the beginning of the poetic dialogue.

> Look, he comes,
>   leaping upon the mountains,
>   bounding over the hills.

> My beloved is like a gazelle
>   or a young stag. (2:8–9)

> How beautiful you are, my love,
>   how very beautiful!
> Your eyes are doves
>   behind your veil.
> Your hair is like a flock of goats,
>   moving down the slopes of Gilead. (4:1)

This connection to wisdom and its base in creation theology helps anchor this poetic drama in the Old Testament's faith tradition.

Daniel

We have noted that the Writings constitute a group of mixed literary types. We have considered most of those. Daniel is also among the Writings, and so we pause here to look at its perspective. Popular interpretations often include Daniel with the Latter Prophets. There are connections with the Prophets, but the form of Daniel is more properly characteristic of apocalyptic literature. The theological approach of this type of literature is that God is the creator and the one who reigns over history. Because of that hope of faith in divine sovereignty, the community can remain faithful and endure the evils of the current age. This literature believes in the culmination of creation in justice. In the categories used in this volume, it tends toward creation theology and certainly operates in revelation of the creator and the response of faithful living discerned in wisdom. The community is called to endure in faithfulness to the one creator, who will bring creation and history to a just culmination. The revelation here is also akin to wisdom in its images and its creation perspective. So I have treated it here as part of the Writings.

Daniel and his companions are endowed with wisdom—"In every matter of wisdom and understanding concerning which the king inquired of them, he found them ten times better than all the magicians and enchanters in his whole kingdom" (1:20)—and chapter 2 portrays Daniel as an interpreter of dreams. The wise Daniel and his friends remain faithful to the one true God, the sovereign over all kingdoms. The narrative is a particular kind of confession of Old Testament creation theology, emphasizing Daniel's wisdom and faithfulness to the sovereign creator. The interplay of creation and covenant theologies is also present in the theological confession of King Darius in 6:25–28. Daniel's God is both liberator and ruler over creation. The visions in the second half of Daniel imagine the creator bringing history and creation to divine good purpose. Such visions of hope give Daniel and his community courage for faithful and wise living.

When considered in the context of the apocalyptic genre, Daniel provides a unified message in both narratives and visions: hope that history will come to its just conclusion. With that hope in place, the community can embrace the fullness of life in this bad time—that is, courageous faithfulness and resistance to idolatry and its attendant lifestyle supported by the Babylonian captors. The message is not unlike that of the Prophets, though its form is different. The emphasis in Daniel is dreams envisioning the fall of the corrupt and oppressive kingdoms of this world and the coming of the kingdom of God, which will not fall. This kingdom will not pass away or be destroyed (7:14). YHWH is the creator, who will bring creation to a just culmination. YHWH calls for righteous living in response to that sure hope. Both creation theology and covenant theology appear in this revelation. The book concludes with an openness as the community awaits the fulfillment of the hope of the kingdom of God, which will not fail, and so embraces a life of faith in the already-but-not-yet.

Conclusion

In the history of scholarship on the theology of the Hebrew Scriptures, the Wisdom literature has not been given sufficient attention. That is primarily because, until recent decades, the paradigm for Old Testament theology has focused on covenant and history, categories into which wisdom does not fit. Wisdom was thus seen as not fitting the norm. I would suggest that the better approach is to include all of the Hebrew canon in a look at the theology of the Hebrew Scriptures and then see what paradigms, if any, are appropriate rather than predetermining a paradigm that excludes part of the canon. This issue leads us back to the matter of the diversity that constitutes the Older Testament and how Old Testament theologians come to terms with that. My view is that wisdom provides a crucial voice in the theology of the Hebrew Scriptures, and I would even suggest that the contemporary setting in which the text is received and interpreted makes wisdom especially critical to hermeneutical and theological conversations.

This chapter has suggested that wisdom operates out of a creation theology. YHWH created the world and placed wisdom in it. He enables sages to observe and learn from creation. In the wisdom texts, sages pass on wisdom to the next generation. Wisdom comes from the creator and is both experiential and universal. It gives considerable attention to the ethical dimensions of the life of faith. Wisdom texts become a means of responding to the revelation of creation theology. Wisdom teaching thus becomes one of the blessings of the creator to make it possible for the community of faith to grow and thrive in the world and in life.

Proverbs is the prime example of pragmatic wisdom, teaching on daily living in God's creation. Proverbs provides literature that is appealing to readers and that leads to reflection on learning and living. Its inclusion in the Hebrew canon suggests that this wisdom comes from the creator, though not all the proverbial sayings are explicit about that. The revelation of wisdom is part of ancient Israel's cultural memory, and this practical wisdom connects that memory with lived experience. The goal and significance of life in this literature is found in healthy community, community shaped by life in line with the created order and with justice. This hope has been given to the human community by the creator so that women and men may celebrate and appreciate the life given by

God. Creation and humanity enjoy and appreciate such culture in the humanities and the sciences, which are part of the creation. Life and the creation are good and to be nurtured in ways appropriate for those created in the image of God, those who are the creator's representatives in caring for the world. The human community experiences these realities in the practical dimensions of life in terms of economics, government, family, work, leisure, various cultural customs, eating, volunteering, sex, relationships, and more. The human task is to enjoy and nurture wholeness of life as God's trusted and responsible creatures. Proverbs as pragmatic wisdom teaches how to respond to the creator, who blesses the creation and the human community with the gifts of life.

Ancient Israel's speculative wisdom texts also come to a number of the central theological struggles of both ancient and modern life as part of the honest dialogue of faith, and in that focus they also connect with the Psalms. Job suffered in severe and undeserved ways. As his story and his dialogue with orthodox wisdom of the day move forward, he moves more profoundly into the mystery of suffering and perceives that the problem of evil and suffering in the world is at the end of the day a theological problem. The creator who rules life and the world eventually condescends to give Job an audience but speaks primarily in questions whose significance is not always obvious to us as readers. Qoheleth also meditates in puzzling ways on the inability of humans to control life and its futures. The human task is to make the most of what the creator, and not humanity, gives. These books of speculative wisdom suggest that the difficult questions and problems of life are also part of faith and worship; otherwise we never move into these issues deeply enough to see some light. So ancient Israel's wisdom movement makes clear that while humans are created for learning, there are limits to human wisdom. Wisdom as a means of response to the revelation of creation is to be desired and sought, with both joy and humility. A wise faith includes struggle with the deepest issues of life. Questions are often the most profound confessions of faith.

This chapter also notes Daniel's hope in the coming and lasting kingdom of God in the face of the community's suffering and oppression.

Its narratives also instruct in wise and faithful living in a context rather different from most of ancient Israel's canon.

Wisdom in this volume's proposal, crafted from the Psalms, is a means of responding to the creator and the blessing of life. Wisdom teaches how to grow and thrive in the creation YHWH has provided. These traditions are treasured and preserved in sanctuaries, synagogues, schools, and homes, and passed on to future generations as part of the story and memory of this faith community. Contemporary communities of faith and persons in those communities can carry forward, live, and teach those memories as they enter that narrative of life and faith.

7

Prophecy

The second division of the Hebrew canon is the Prophets, which is composed of the Former Prophets, discussed in chapter 4, and the Latter Prophets, the subject to which we now turn. The Latter Prophets consists of four prophetic books—Isaiah, Jeremiah, Ezekiel, and the Book of the Twelve. In Protestantism, these are simply labeled "the Prophets," with the first three as the Major Prophets and the Twelve with the unfortunate label of the Minor Prophets. We will find that prophetic theology dominates all these books.

In prophetic theology, God speaks proclamations of judgment and hope and calls for a response of repentance. Prophecy combines the theological perspectives of creation and covenant and makes a new beginning in portraying YHWH as the God who speaks and calls for repentance in response. That theological distinction reflects a literary distinction of prophetic books in comparison with other parts of the Hebrew canon, yet these books are also closely connected to the rest of that canon. In the Latter Prophets, Isaiah's prophetic theology connects to the Davidic covenant, Jeremiah's connects to the Sinaitic covenant, and Ezekiel's to Priestly theology. The Twelve embraces creation and covenant theologies at various points in the context of the genre of prophecy in which YHWH speaks messages of judgment and hope.

Judgment oracles respond to injustice and idolatry in the community. Hope oracles are based in divine fidelity to the relationship with Israel and anticipate a human response of faithfulness to that relationship. Prophetic oracles and prophetic books declare the divine message to the community.

Traditionally the prophetic books are treated chronologically, beginning with Amos. Such treatments are organized by way of historical concerns or historical-critical methods. Theological treatments of these texts of necessity interact with such issues but in this volume are not controlled by them. Rather, the approach here is literary and theological. Our look at the prophetic corpus will then take clues from the Protestant canon of the Older Testament and treat the four prophetic scrolls in order—Isaiah, Jeremiah, Ezekiel, and the Twelve—following the ancient tradition of seeing the Twelve as constituting one scroll with various parts. We will see that each of the four books contains considerable diversity.

Isaiah

The vision of Isaiah is a lengthy prophetic tradition related to various sociohistorical settings in the life of ancient Israel. The prophetic tradition calls on creation and covenant theologies to hold the community accountable for their relationship with the divine and with each other—often related to the Davidic covenant traditions in the book's early chapters—and to speak powerful images of hope for a defeated community. God speaks powerfully through the prophet of both judgment and hope. A return to wise and faithful living is the prophetic goal; therein is a glorious promise. The call is to turn from unfaith, whether it be in the form of injustice and idolatry or in the form of disbelief in the liberating and blessing divine activity and presence.

The opening chapter of the book introduces the prophet's preaching. The opening proclamation indicts the community for covenant infidelity in their relationship with YHWH. Zion is central in these texts and a symbol of the community of YHWH. The prophet proclaims that worship in Zion must be tied to social justice. The current covenant

infidelity of the people has become a major threat to Zion, leaving a
besieged city as a result. The prophet pleads for fidelity to the relationship with the covenant Lord YHWH.

> Wash yourselves; make yourselves clean;
>> remove the evil of your doings
>> from before my eyes;
> cease to do evil,
>> learn to do good;
> seek justice,
>> rescue the oppressed,
> defend the orphan,
>> plead for the widow. (1:16–17)

That kind of repentance will make possible a hopeful future in contrast to the death encountered in injustice and infidelity. The powerless
(orphan and widow) will find ways forward in life. The opening chapter exemplifies the strong language of prophetic proclamations in the
Older Testament, portraying Zion as a shockingly corrupt community
in need of the painful refining fire that judgment brings. The prophet
seeks fidelity and hope.

> Zion shall be redeemed by justice,
>> and those in her who repent, by righteousness. (1:27)

This picture of repentance characterizes the righteous remnant as
those who cling to right relationship with YHWH worked out in right
relationship with the community. Such is the call of the prophet to a
community that apparently lacks the ability to understand. Chapter
2 then provides a marvelous picture of the prophet's hope, with many
peoples coming to Zion to learn YHWH's instruction for living. The
structure of divine revelation and human response shapes the poetry. The
proclamation is judgment, and the response of repentance brings hope.

We have noted in previous chapters that the defeat of Jerusalem in
the sixth century by Babylon was an unrivaled trauma for Judah. Their

center did not hold, and life as they had known it ceased to exist. The king was gone, and so there was no hope for justice; the temple was gone, and so there was no hope for atonement. The prophetic tradition of Isaiah spoke to this crisis in eloquent poetry announcing good news for exiles: there will be a second exodus. As God brought Israel out of Egypt, God will bring Israel out of Babylon. So the prophetic proclamation here centers on hope. This part of the book begins in chapter 40 with the call to comfort the people because their trauma of exile is over. The Persian ruler Cyrus is now the dominant ruler in Mesopotamia, and he will act as YHWH's chosen one to make it possible for the remnant of Judah to return to Jerusalem. The creator will strengthen the powerless. This proclamation combines the theological perspectives of YHWH as both liberator and creator. The creator will do a new thing and liberate the remnant from exile. The prophet seeks to convince the defeated community of this hope, debating with them, putting their doubts on trial, and proclaiming oracles of salvation. The return from exile will reveal the glory of the Lord, who is present and active in the world. This combining of creation and covenant theology brilliantly characterizes the prophetic corpus.

> Do not fear, for I am with you;
>   I will bring your offspring from the east,
>   and from the west I will gather you;
> I will say to the north, "Give them up,"
>   and to the south, "Do not withhold;
> bring my sons from far away
>   and my daughters from the end of the earth—
> everyone who is called by my name,
>   whom I created for my glory,
>   whom I formed and made." (43:5–7)

Isaiah 40–55 focuses on a word of hope for exiles by prophesying a second exodus from exile. Chapter 40 begins precisely with a word of comfort that the community's imprisonment is at an end. And yet, as we read the chapter, it is the language of creation that portrays the God who will deliver and bless. The creation language is explicit at the end of the chapter. The creator in these chapters will do something new and calls for the community to sing a new song, reminiscent of the Psalms' tradition of the reign of YHWH, for the creator is present to bless those who will come out of exile. In these chapters YHWH is the one who delivers and the one who blesses, redeemer and creator; the traditions are inseparably intertwined. The prophetic genre is important for the interweaving of the traditions. Isaiah is made up of prophecies, proclamations in which YHWH speaks to the community, in Isaiah 40–55 calling for the dispirited community to turn from despair to hope. Chapters 56–66 continue to call the discouraged community to hope in the face of despair.

Jeremiah

The dominant strain of Jeremiah's theological language is indebted to the covenant tradition and especially emphasizes covenant fidelity in response to the covenant God. This covenant God offers the gift of prophetic speech, which calls the people to wholeness of life by way of turning to covenant keeping, the path of full life. Right relationship with the covenant God is both gift and task. Jeremiah proclaims that the people have presumed on the gift and corrupted the task. The goal is wholeness of life found in covenant keeping. The prophet calls for repentance of the community and of persons, a turning which will move them from judgment to hope. Jeremiah includes both the community as a whole and individuals in this call. He seems to emphasize the individual a bit more than previous parts of the Older Testament. The call is to turn away from a life of injustice, idolatry, and evil—a path leading to destruction and death—and to turn toward a life of justice, faithfulness, and right relationship with YHWH demonstrated in right relationship with others. Such a faithful life leads to integrity and wholeness.

While Jeremiah includes references to creation traditions and images, with YHWH as the one who reigns over all, covenant theology remains dominant. Jeremiah 7 is an account of the temple sermon. The people have come to view the temple as a good luck charm that will always shield them from trouble and bring them the good things of life. Jeremiah calls them to live rather in covenant fidelity and hope by caring for the widow and orphan and immigrant. Such repentance shapes the hope of deliverance for the covenant community.

Jeremiah's prophecies become more hopeful beyond the defeat of conquest and exile. Perhaps the promise of a new covenant, a new internal way to create a covenant community, in chapter 31 is the most familiar. The new covenant is still a relationship initiated by YHWH and focused on *torah*, but YHWH will write the *torah* in the hearts of the people, the seat of decision for them. Covenant faithfulness is central to Jeremiah's proclamation, and this text is a creative contribution to that message in a context of community trauma. Jeremiah has been characterized as the grieving prophet, grieving over the sin of the people and its consequences.

Ezekiel

The prophecy of Ezekiel is a powerful and puzzling proclamation of the divine message to a community traumatized by the death of their world and life together. YHWH speaks to this traumatized community in unusual ways because the worst is yet to come in the fall of their holy city and temple. But beyond this judgment there is hope for a renewed life. In the latter part of Ezekiel 37, following the vision of the valley of dry bones, the prophet characterizes this hope in terms of a renewed covenant with a Davidic king ruling. "My dwelling place shall be with them; and I will be their God, and they shall be my people" (37:27). The concluding section envisions a cleansed and renewed temple with the divine presence as the sign of a future beyond the exile. Throughout the book, YHWH continues to be present and active and speaking so that the people "will know that I am YHWH."

This scroll illustrates the combination of both creation and covenant theologies. Accusations of idolatry suggest covenant breaking, and the hope of renewing the relationship with YHWH rests on covenant keeping. These theological emphases on idolatry and covenant renewal in Ezekiel's prophecies partake of the long-standing tradition of the formation of the covenant community by YHWH and the hope of their embodying covenant instruction. Ezekiel was also a priest, focused on the temple in terms of clean and unclean. We have seen in earlier chapters that these priestly perspectives partake of creation theology and the God who is present to bless. The prophet's hope is for the community to have a renewed relationship with the creator and covenant God. The prophet combines creation and covenant emphases in ways that are difficult to separate. The distinction of the prophet is that God here speaks to the exilic community messages of judgment and of hope tied to the defeat of Jerusalem. The needed response is a turning from idolatry to faithfulness in worship and wisdom in living. The prophecies of Ezekiel are a full-blown example of contextual theology. The form of a number of them is particularly problematic in the context of the twenty-first century. They exhibit extreme language, form, and imagery for an extreme and traumatic setting. They are often culturally conditioned and so will not be favorite choices for contemporary interpretation. When carefully interpreted, however, they do contribute to Old Testament theology in speaking to a difficult time.

The Twelve

We will consider the Twelve as the fourth scroll of the Latter Prophets and thus as a unity or anthology that comprises twelve parts. It is important to read each part or book carefully and also to read the whole. The parts are connected, and the twelve parts make a diversity of contributions to the whole. The whole emphasizes the consequences of the community's wickedness but also hope for the future, an important theological perspective. The theological traditions of creation and covenant are intertwined in the Twelve with a clear emphasis on the community's response to such divine initiative. The beginnings and endings of the twelve parts are similar, and we will note further connections as we consider the parts. Hosea appears first.

Hosea

Hosea serves as a messenger delivering a message from YHWH about fidelity in the covenant relationship. The center of the message is at the heart of covenant theology in the Older Testament. YHWH created this covenant community and is committed to the people. The message calls the community to faithfulness in covenant living, as opposed to being seduced by false promises of idolatrous fertility religions. The audience of Hosea (and of the Twelve) is called to decide about Israel's history and its import for the present.

> Those who are wise understand these things;
>   those who are discerning know them.
> For the ways of the LORD are right,
>   and the upright walk in them,
>   but transgressors stumble in them. (14:9)

Hosea vividly calls the community to faithfulness in their relationship with YHWH in the final declining years of the Northern Kingdom. The proclamation begins with YHWH's love for Israel, and the YHWH-Israel "marriage" becomes the primary metaphor for the prophet's message. Because fullness of life comes only by way of YHWH, the prophet speaks of divine jealousy as a way of saying that YHWH is zealous for Israel to encounter wholeness in life and that that only comes in keeping covenant with YHWH. The prophet thus speaks harshly of syncretism and rails against the leaders who have brought the community toward the fertility religion of the Baals with empty promises of prosperity. Israel's idolatry is adultery in relationship with YHWH. Hosea calls for the community to return to the wilderness and the time of the beginning of the relationship with YHWH to renew a relationship characterized by covenant keeping.

The prophecy also reflects creation theology in its account of the consequences of this covenant breaking. The creator has blessed this community with the land and its creatures and the sea and its creatures. Even the creation suffers from the folly of infidelity to this creator and liberator.

> Therefore the land mourns,
>> and all who live in it languish;
> together with the wild animals
>> and the birds of the air,
>> even the fish of the sea are perishing. (4:3)

Hosea portrays YHWH as both just and tender and indeed as a God who is in anguish about the community's infidelity. The prophecy calls the people to renewal of their relationship with YHWH, using the language of repentance in the concluding chapter. The divine graciousness makes a future hope possible for the community and for creation beyond the judgment at hand (Hosea 11; 14). Hosea speaks in YHWH's stead and calls for covenant fidelity and wise living; such actions constitute repentance.

Joel

The brief prophecy of Joel begins with a lament over a severe locust plague that is a sign of the coming day of YHWH. The prophecy calls for repentance, and the latter part of the text turns to hope found in faithfulness to YHWH. The day of YHWH in the end is hopeful. The cultic tradition of lament is central to Joel's call for fidelity and hope. The brief collection of prophecies follows a three-part pattern seen in other prophetic texts: judgment on Judah and Jerusalem followed by judgment on the nations followed by words of hope for the future. The prophetic word of Joel combines covenant theology and creation theology, with considerable use of creation language, as with the locust plague, and with covenant language focused on the repentance in the relationship with YHWH that brings a future of hope in YHWH as refuge. Joel's messages of judgment and hope place this book firmly in the context of prophetic theology: "The LORD roars from Zion, and utters his voice from Jerusalem" (3:16). That verse connects to the next book, Amos, which uses the same poetic line to introduce the divine word to the community (Amos 1:2).

Amos

The message of Amos is that the day of YHWH is at hand and will
be a day of justice and accountability for Israel. Judgment is coming
because of oppression of the poor, a corrupt legal system, and corruption in the religious life of the community. The day of YHWH
is important in the Older Testament and particularly in the Latter
Prophets. It is the day of divine victory and divine rule and means
trouble for YHWH's enemies. But for Amos, Israel is strikingly among
those who are YHWH's enemies because of the corruption in the life
they have been given.

> You only have I known
>   of all the families of the earth;
> therefore I will punish you
>   for all your iniquities. (3:2)

The Latter Prophets are primarily concerned with two kinds of sin:
social injustice and idolatry. With Amos the central matter is social
injustice and thus the terms of justice and righteousness in 5:24. Righteousness indicates a divine-human relationship, initiated by God and
demonstrated in right relationships with humans. A just society cares
for its people. Amos declares that Israel has forgotten that YHWH
provides for all the members of the community. Many contemporary
readers may well think of justice in retributive terms, but the Latter
Prophets understand social justice as a theological matter. YHWH
delivers ancient Israel and calls this community to embody a right
relationship with YHWH in right human relationships, relationships
of justice and integrity. The prophetic understanding of justice begins
with the injunction for the community to see that all of its members
have what is needed for completeness of life because God has provided
life for the community. To see that all have what they need for a full
life characterizes the prophetic view of justice and defines what Amos
means by the term. Judgment on injustice is at the heart of prophetic
theology as a call for covenant fidelity.

International diplomacy provides the background for the understanding of prophets as messengers. As a diplomatic messenger receives from a king a message to be brought to another king, Amos receives a message from YHWH and delivers it to the people: thus says the Lord. Amos calls the covenant community to a life of justice; that is what characterizes a faithful covenant community. The rhetoric of this formative eighth-century prophet is reminiscent of Abraham Joshua Heschel's image of the prophet as one screaming into a loudspeaker. Many interpreters have seen it as a word of doom and gloom. The prophecies of judgment are calls to repentance, calls to turn to a life of justice as the essential living-out of a faithful relationship with YHWH, who is both deliverer and creator. Language of creation runs through the book from its first verse to its last, especially in the doxologies, which depict God as the creator (4:13; 5:8–9; 9:5–6). Furthermore, Amos opens with prophecies of judgment on the nations. The creator is God of all nations and calls all peoples to live both justly and wisely.

Amos alludes to covenant tradition with the reference to *torah* in 2:4 and with the exodus reference in 2:10. Chapter 3 begins with an allusion to the deliverance from Egypt and the responsibility it brings for those in relationship with the covenant God YHWH. Amos 9:7–8 refers to the exodus from Egypt but does so amid a portrayal of God as the one who delivers also the Philistines and Arameans. The opening of the oracles against the nations in Amos 1–2 focuses on nations surrounding Israel and Judah, with the implication that God as the creator of all has expectations of all peoples. The prophecies in Amos include several references to worship of the God who roars from Zion (1:2), a tradition that is part of the perspective of creation theology in the Older Testament connected to the temple and to Zion. It is the creator (4:13; 5:8–9; 9:5–6) who brings judgment on the foolish house of Israel. And the book comes to a striking conclusion with the use of the language of creation and portrays the God who comes to bless in the word of hope beyond judgment. While Amos does not regularly use the explicit vocabulary of covenant, the prophecies clearly understand that the covenant God YHWH has created this community of Israel and calls for the people to live faithfully in that relationship—that is, to live in justice and righteousness with others in the community. The book also uses the language of wisdom (3:3–8) to call the community to hear the message of YHWH (3:1; 4:1; 5:1) and seek YHWH and live fully and do what is right. Amos combines creation and covenant traditions and does so in ways that make it difficult to separate the traditions. The distinctive of Amos is that here God speaks: thus says the Lord. The human response called for in light of this revelation is to turn (repent) from injustice and unfaith to justice and faith. That is the heart of prophetic theology.

Obadiah

Obadiah reflects the experience of exile and follows a three-part pattern seen in other prophetic texts. In this case, judgment has come on Israel and Jerusalem and will come on the nations, especially Edom, who betrayed brother Israel as Babylon was besieging Jerusalem. The Edomites were descendants of Esau and so should have related to Jacob/Israel in a brotherly way. Judgment will come to Edom (the day of the Lord), and hope will come to Israel. Obadiah is among the prophetic voices that interpret the trauma of defeat and exile for the community and seek to help the people envision a future hope, a renewal of the kingdom of YHWH. Despite its brevity, Obadiah includes the primary elements of prophetic theology—judgment, hope—as a proclamation of the one who is both creator and deliverer.

Jonah

Rather than preserving the prophet's oracles, Jonah recounts the narrative of its namesake and so is distinct from other prophetic books. The message of the book makes clear that YHWH cares for all of creation and for all creatures in it. In this book, Jonah speaks a divine message to Nineveh, but YHWH speaks to the Jewish community by way of the character Jonah to call for repentance from a narrow theological viewpoint to one that embraces all creation as the concern of YHWH and the realm of divine presence and blessing. Repentance is possible even for wicked Nineveh. The book functions like a parable, with the last chapter pressing its point by way of the dialogue between Jonah and YHWH.

The significance of the prophetic short story is that the creator who reigns does not support the exclusive or particularist approach of some parts of the Jewish community but instead cares for all of creation. With the story's emphasis on repentance and the allusion in chapter 4 to the confession of faith in Exodus 34, the book of Jonah certainly relates to covenant traditions in the Older Testament and hope of deliverance from judgment. At the same time, with the sea, the great fish, the repentance of Nineveh, and the plant, creation traditions are also front and center in the book, all in the context of a proclamation from this prophetic figure.

Micah

Micah proclaims that a theophany is coming and will bring judgment because of false prophets, corrupt courts, and rapacious leaders. Injustice is central to this prophecy. The book is organized by way of a judgment-hope pattern and sees hope for a remnant. Micah 6:1–8 is a brief but powerful summary of the preaching of the eighth-century prophets Amos, Hosea, Isaiah, and Micah. The accusation is that the people offer empty sacrifices not reflected in the community's life. The covenant God YHWH calls for all the community to live in justice.

> He has told you, O mortal, what is good;
>> and what does the LORD require of you
> but to do justice, and to love kindness,
>> and to walk humbly with your God? (6:8)

The call is to right relationship with YHWH lived out in right relationships with humans. Micah speaks for YHWH as the creator who comes in theophany and who seeks covenant fidelity.

Nahum

When compared with Jeremiah's or Zephaniah's word to Judah at a similar time, Nahum's address to seventh-century Judah shows the diversity
of the prophetic tradition. YHWH who speaks in Nahum is both creator
and redeemer, calling the Judean community to turn from despondency
in the face of oppression to hope in YHWH. Nahum's message is that
YHWH reigns and will in the end bring justice on the wicked Assyrian
capital. Assyria had long oppressed Judah and other peoples; in that
sense Nahum is a word of hope for the oppressed. The proclamation is
that YHWH the creator seeks relationships centered on justice.

Habakkuk

The prophecy of Habakkuk is about divine justice. The book takes
the form of the cultic tradition of lament as a way to shape a dialogue
between the prophet and God on the justice of God. For example, the
opening lament focuses on how YHWH can continue to allow injustice and unrighteousness to prevail. The response is that Babylon will
become the instrument of divine justice. The book concludes with an
assurance of YHWH's justice and fidelity. The call is to trust in divine
justice. Creation language runs through the brief book, though the
primary theological perspective is the covenant tradition that YHWH is
the divine liberator who will in justice renew the covenant community
in the face of ongoing oppression.

Zephaniah

In Zephaniah, the reasons for judgment include both idolatry and social
injustice, but there is hope for restoration for a remnant, a perspective
reminiscent of Isaiah. YHWH speaks here on the basis of the reign
of YHWH, which will manifest itself on the day of the Lord in all of
creation. The book concludes in hymnic rejoicing over divine justice
bringing blessing for fullness of life. The victorious creator brings justice for the righteous remnant. The prophetic poetry of Zephaniah
combines the perspectives of creation and covenant theologies in ways

that are inseparable. The covenant God who reigns over all of creation comes to deliver.

> I will deal with all your oppressors
>> at that time.
> And I will save the lame
>> and gather the outcast,
> and I will change their shame into praise
>> and renown in all the earth. (3:19)

Haggai

Haggai encourages the people to move ahead with the rebuilding of the temple so that the divine presence will be manifest with the people when they worship in Jerusalem. The prophetic hope is both a renewal of the covenant people and a renewal of divine presence with the people by way of the rebuilt temple, yet again interweaving covenant and creation perspectives in this prophetic proclamation. The wise response to this revelation is fidelity to the divine-human relationship in this struggling community.

Zechariah

The renewal of the reign of the creator is central to Zechariah's theological perspective. The verse known from the New Testament rejoices in the reign of the creator.

> Rejoice greatly, O daughter of Zion!
>> Shout aloud, O daughter of Jerusalem!
> Lo, your king comes to you;
>> triumphant and victorious is he,
> humble and riding on a donkey,
>> on a colt, the foal of a donkey. (9:9)

The book begins with a call to repentance, and so covenant themes are also present.

Thus says the LORD of hosts: Return to me, says the LORD of hosts, and I will return to you, says the LORD of hosts. Do not be like your ancestors, to whom the former prophets proclaimed, "Thus says the LORD of hosts, Return from your evil ways and from your evil deeds." (1:3–4)

Prophecy takes the form of warning and calls the hearers to new paths, as it often does in the Hebrew Bible.

Malachi

Malachi operates from the covenant traditions (3:5, 14, 18; 4:4) and emphasizes both cult and family as the means of passing faith on to the next generations. These institutions also have some connection to creation themes (1:5, 14; 2:10). The book preserves six oracles that emphasize the love of YHWH for Israel and the hope that Israel will respond to this love in covenant faithfulness. Malachi speaks of the divine pathos, YHWH's hope and work to renew the covenant relationship so that the people can embrace the fullness of life and the blessings of the creator. The prophet is concerned about inadequate sacrifices the priests are accepting and about the ending of marriages for the purpose of finding a better family arrangement for economic reasons. The prophet is also concerned about the loss of hope in the struggling community in the aftermath of exile; the people have little faith in divine justice. There is apparently a good bit of skepticism and discouragement about divine-human engagement in this community, and the prophet speaks to that setting. The prophecy calls for faithful living in this time of looking forward to the day of YHWH, which will bring justice as the covenant promises. The community's response to the prophet's challenging oracles will determine whether the future holds blessing or cursing.

--- **Conclusion** ---

The Latter Prophets operated in a context we considered previously with the Former Prophets. These prophetic figures from the time of the monarchy were central in holding the community accountable with the shift to kingship as the central institution of the society. They persistently raised the question of faithfulness to the creator and covenant God. This move to a more diversified and consumer-oriented society was difficult in itself. It carried theological implications in terms of a tendency toward Canaanite culture with its idols and toward injustice in the oppression of others in order to gain more possessions. Canaanite fertility religion promised prosperity in all arenas. Social injustice and idolatry brought strong prophecies of judgment against corruption of the creation and breaking of the covenant. The Latter Prophets maintained at the same time the divine initiative toward hope and justice in the divine-human relationship. Divine fidelity to that relationship called for human fidelity in response. The prophets spoke of judgment and of hope for renewing the divine-human relationship beyond the corruption of the current context. It was the destruction of Jerusalem that constituted the most extreme trauma in the life of the ancient community. The Latter Prophets served as interpreters of this disaster. What had happened? What about the future? What about YHWH? Chaos was now at the door. Life as they had known it was no more—without king or temple. There was no center. Prophets articulated the grief in major texts such as Jeremiah and Ezekiel, and the aftermath of exile is palpably present in Haggai and Malachi, for example. The prophetic literature is a major achievement in seeking to come to terms with this trauma. The prophets of the sixth and fifth centuries BCE brought significant voices to the troubled era.

The Latter Prophets begins with three major prophetic voices, formative figures from the eighth, seventh, and sixth centuries BCE. Isaiah called for a sure faith around the Assyrian threat, and hopes relating to Isaiah's proclamation in the midst of the later exile and its aftermath continued to shape that prophetic scroll. Davidic covenant emphases are central to the scroll. Jeremiah is a profound interpreter of the capture by the Babylonians and helped to envision a future beyond that trauma. Jeremiah is a proclaimer of the Sinaitic covenant. Ezekiel interprets exile and a hope beyond it by way of his priestly tradition and the departure of the divine presence from an unclean temple and the return of the presence to a new temple. The scroll of Ezekiel is troubling and difficult at times, but such was his time and task. The Twelve includes prophetic voices from the deadly path toward defeat through the trauma of exile and on to the hope for a future beyond this conflagration. It is an anthology of voices from these social settings linked together by common language and themes—a unity that promises a future with YHWH and offers guidance for that life together. This prophetic corpus offers both judgment and hope: judgment on the sins of idolatry and social injustice and hope beyond the consequences of these ways of infidelity. YHWH continues in fidelity, speaks to the community by way of these prophetic voices, and demonstrates the divine pathos in going with the community in defeat and in liberation.

The prophetic corpus strikingly combines creation and covenant perspectives in a new literary guise, that of prophecy, in which God speaks and calls for repentance in response, for a turning to fidelity and justice for the life of faith. This distinctive constitutes a theological perspective for prophetic theology. In the important temple sermon, Jeremiah calls the people to amend their ways (7:5–7), and in chapter 18 YHWH as the potter calls, "Turn now, all of you from your evil way, and amend your ways and your doings" (v. 11). Hosea 14:1 calls the people to return or repent; Malachi 3:7 calls the community to return to YHWH. The divine revelation and human response in prophetic theology is God's speaking and humans' repenting, whether in the face of judgment or in hope. These prophecies become part of the script people of faith carry with them in the memory of living poetry as they move in conversation with the script and shape their own narratives.

8

Conclusion

This volume has explored the theology of the Older Testament in order to help students and other interested readers make a start in exploring the subject as a further dive into the significance of the Old Testament for faith. This exploration has revealed that the subject has become extraordinarily complicated. It is a conundrum, and that context glares at all of us who would explore the subject. Some would say that we should call a halt to the exploration. They consider it a futile effort that will bring no fruit. We can continue to explore Old Testament texts, they say, and even ask theological questions of them, but to work at the structure and method of Old Testament theology as a subject has been rendered of no good value. So why have I continued to explore this subject? I have suggested that the study of any literary-theological document is inevitably tied to frameworks. Readers interpret texts from a framework. Individual texts relate in some way to a larger framework—a biblical chapter or book or testament—and that larger framework looms as a frame to structure interpretations of the text. The part relates to the whole. The framework or structure of the theology of the Hebrew Scriptures is an essential part of any exploration of these texts. This framework or shape of Old Testament theology is heuristic. It does not determine everything about understanding the text, nor does it solve all the questions of interpretation. Still, it provides starting points, frameworks to explore the subject in ways meaningful to readers. So in this volume I seek to provide a framework to make it possible for students to read and interpret the Hebrew Bible in more meaningful and life-giving ways.

The framework proposed herein begins with the thesis that these texts circle around questions tied to divine-human engagements. Those engagements begin with divine revelation and elicit human responses. The dialogue of divine revelation and human response pervades the various literatures of the Old Testament, and I have proposed three primary perspectives of this revelation-and-response nexus reflected in these texts. The analogy I have called on is that of three legs of a stool, a tripos. The three legs are creation theology, covenant theology, and prophetic theology.

> In *creation theology*, YHWH is present to bless, to empower a community and a world to grow and thrive. This life-giving divine power is present to provide all the things of creation that make everyday life possible. Central to Genesis is the portrayal of the divine as one who is present to bless, to make life possible in creation. And how should the human community, created as the image of God, respond to this power of creation? By seeking to learn the wisdom God has woven into the creation and living by that wisdom. Therein is found shalom, an integrity for life in which the pieces fit the whole in ways that bring growth and hope.
>
> The second leg of the stool is *covenant theology*. What is covenant? It is a relationship in which YHWH calls, "I will be your God," and Israel responds, "Yes, and we will be your people." The defining narrative for this perspective is the story of the exodus from Egypt. Here ancient Israel takes initiative in the midst of great suffering and cries to God for deliverance. YHWH hears their cry and comes to deliver in great and mighty acts of many kinds. Covenant theology begins with the divine move to deliver from great trouble to a new community in relationship with the

covenant God and with each other. So how is this community to respond to such a deliverance? The community responds in living by *torah*, God's covenant instruction in how to embody this relationship. Much of the Pentateuch specifies the shape of this *torah*, calling for worship of YHWH and love of fellow humans.

And the third leg of the tripos is *prophetic theology*, in which YHWH speaks through prophetic figures and urges the community to live as faithful gardeners of the creation and as just keepers of the covenant. The creation and covenant perspectives are interwoven inseparably and communicated by messengers in ways that call the community to repentance, to turn from injustice and lack of faith to wise and just living to bring the community back to a life of integrity. This prophetic theology, with its call to repentance, is primarily instantiated in the four books of the Latter Prophets: Isaiah, Jeremiah, Ezekiel, and the Twelve.

These three theological perspectives provide *a* (not *the*) framing device to account for much of the theological dimension of the Older Testament. The three legs support the seat of the stool, fullness of life for all of creation, humanity, and community. I will return to this issue shortly.

Divine-human engagement in terms of revelation and response and these three theological perspectives of creation, covenant, and prophetic theologies are at the heart of the framework I am proposing for understanding the theology of the Older Testament. Such a theological frame provides important context for those who seek to understand the Old Testament in theological ways. But there is more. There is also the matter of how one proceeds in exploring the theology of the Hebrew Scriptures. The significance of texts comes to reality in the interchange between text and readers. I have suggested that the literary shape of texts offers guidance to readers. The text has already embedded in it the intentions of its originators and their cultural codes. Readers include all these dimensions of texts in order to understand/interpret the text. For readers with theological purposes, questions of literary type come into play. Forms of narrative and of poetry are significant in the Older Testament. Communities of readers can enter narratives and embody them, and the narratives become part of cultural memory that shapes theological and ethical perspectives. The sound and imagery of poetry work in a similar way to capture human imagination and shape life together. In the introduction we noted the view of James Gustafson that narratives shape communities and characters for living. I would add that poetic texts also become part of community memories to that end.

But even prior to these hermeneutical processes is the question of the shape of divine-human engagement in the Hebrew Bible, the three perspectives of creation, covenant, and prophetic theologies. These do not spring de novo from the imagination but rather come from the textual starting point of the Psalms, the most representative Old Testament confession of the ancient worshiping community's faith. Chapter 2 articulated a rationale for beginning with the Psalter as "Israel's creed" sung by the congregation. The chorus is the memories of YHWH as the one who blesses, delivers, and speaks, calling humans to remember wisdom, follow covenant instruction, and embody justice (repentance) in the Yahwistic tradition. This sung creed provides a textual shape to the theological perspectives in Old Testament narrative and poetry as a frame for exploring the theological import of the Old Testament. This volume has sought to articulate these contexts so that readers can begin to explore the various parts of the Hebrew canon with these theological perspectives in mind. The volume has then provided hints of these perspectives in parts of the canon.

Much of Genesis, from the creation accounts through the ancestral narratives, operates from a creation theology in which YHWH is present to bless, to make it possible for the human community and all of creation to grow and thrive. The call to the human community is to learn the wisdom God gives and live by it. Much of Exodus and of the remainder of the Pentateuch in a variety of ways and contexts operates from a covenant theology in which God hears the cry of an oppressed community and comes to deliver and bring the community into a covenant relationship in which *torah* is taught as a guide for life together.

The Former Prophets base their theological perspective on the covenant theology of Deuteronomy, in which YHWH has brought Israel together as a covenant community and given them life to shape together in faith and in justice. In the Psalms, a covenant context is central to prayer and to the historical accounts of divine deliverance in the psalms of praise. Creation theology is formative for many of the hymns of praise. Prophetic theology also makes an appearance in the theological drama of the Psalter. The primary Wisdom texts in the Old Testament relate to creation theology and the wisdom the creator has given to creatures. The Latter Prophets interweave both creation and covenant perspectives in a variety of ways with the perspective that YHWH speaks through these messengers and calls for repentance leading to wise and just lives. Prophets speak in contexts in which the community has lost its way. Repentance calls for a return to justice and hope.

Another part of our current interpretive context is the history of the discipline of Old Testament theology. That history really necessitates such a framework for readers. A brief summary makes clear that what we think of today as the academic subject of Old Testament theology is an invention of modernity. From the time of Gabler's famous lecture in 1787, Old Testament theology has been separated from dogmatic theology and taken its own path. The major developments came in the twentieth century. Eichrodt's work in the 1930s emphasized the structure of the theology of the Older Testament and found its center to be "covenant." Von Rad followed in the middle of the twentieth century with an alternative emphasis on the variety of theological traditions in the Hebrew Scriptures and their connections to ancient Israel's historical experience. It was in the last third of the twentieth century that Brevard Childs entered the discussion with a renewed emphasis on canon as the context of exegesis and theological reflection. This emphasis marks a move away from history as the basis for theological reflection on texts in the Hebrew Scriptures. At the end of the twentieth century, Walter Brueggemann published what some have characterized as the first postmodern Old Testament theology, a metaphorical theology that uses the image of a courtroom to present the considerable variety of witnesses articulating ancient Israel's faith. Work on the structure and method of Old Testament theology has continued in the last two decades in the context of the multiple theological traditions present in the Old Testament.

Historically, scholars have thus begun with the text of the Hebrew Scriptures, emphasized the organization of theological reflection on these texts, and come to see the diversity involved, and yet without attention to the shape of the Hebrew canon and the question of how to present the faith perspectives comprehensibly in our contemporary context. A serious conundrum with the current state of the discipline is that a realistic characterization of it is Leo Perdue's "shattered spectrum." There is precious little agreement on the frameworks in which we work or on where to start or how to proceed. Is the search for a shape for Old Testament theology a futile effort?

I have above argued that frameworks and structures are important for interpretive work and so worth the effort. At the same time, we must admit that the "shattered spectrum" is an apt portrayal of the current state of the theology of the Older Testament. In that context, we as interpreters look for a place to begin and a way to proceed in presenting a shape for the theology of the Hebrew Bible that provides a heuristic starting point so that we can continue to explore the theological import of these texts. I have suggested that the place to begin is in the text itself and, in particular, the book of Psalms as the ancient community's confession of faith. That confession suggests three theological perspectives of divine revelation and human response in the divine-human engagement the Psalms portray: creation theology with the response by way of wisdom, covenant theology with the response by way of *torah*, and prophetic theology with the response by way of repentance. In the context of that framework, I then proceeded through the Hebrew canon to explore these theological perspectives in the Older Testament. These chapters are but hints of how these perspectives both inform and are reflected in the Hebrew text. The hope of this volume is that its readers will spend much time now exploring these theological reflections in these rich and mysterious texts.

Several of the advantages to the approach this volume takes to Old Testament theology relate to the history of the discipline recounted in chapter 1. The question of a starting point for the discipline makes a difference, and a textual starting point is a strength. The case for beginning with the Psalms moves the narrative ahead, and the Psalms provide various perspectives for readers. It is also important to note the diversity among the three theological perspectives engaged in this volume. The Old Testament is clearly not only a covenant theology book. The history of the discipline has recovered the significance of creation. The covenant emphasis has also pushed wisdom to the side in the discussion of the shape of Old Testament theology. The proposal here gives wisdom its rightful place. Creation and covenant are significant in the Hebrew Bible. I believe the case for the importance of prophetic theology is also strong; it is a major portion of the canon. It is also important that these three perspectives can interact. Creation and covenant are interwoven in the Latter Prophets, and we have noted other instances of that interaction. The covenant theology operative in the story of Esther and creation theology operative in the story of Ruth also illustrate the diversity of perspectives in this shape of Old Testament theology. Both originate in the Second Temple period. Esther emphasizes covenant theology in which God will at all costs preserve (deliver) the Jewish community. Ruth is about the blessing of the creator to be shared with all people. These perspectives are in one sense two sides of one coin, the divine-human engagement. At times a diversity of perspectives fits a diversity of contexts, but at other times, a diversity of theological perspectives provides a fuller view of divine revelation and human response. The variety of perspectives is not contradictory but is a more holistic approach.

I have used the analogy of the three-legged stool of the Cambridge tripos as a way to present these three theological perspectives as the three legs of the stool. I have mentioned the seat of the stool supported by the three legs but not said too much about that. I am keenly aware that the stool is an analogy. One of my seminary homiletics professors was fond of saying that every analogy limps along like a three-legged table! This stool is not missing a leg, but the stool is an analogy, as is its seat. The seat is not a static thing. I have labeled it "salvation," but some would see that term as essentially a covenant term tied to deliverance. Others would tie it to deliverance from this life and its earthly existence. I use the term in relation to its Latin origin. It is tied to fullness, wholeness, completeness, or healing. It is akin to the Hebrew sense of integrity. The parts of life fit together as a whole in the divine-human engagement. Salvation in that sense is YHWH's hope for our life together, and the variety of theological perspectives of revelation and response make that hope possible for us. I don't want to say too much about the seat of the stool. I hope you will explore that avenue.

I conclude with the starting place for this project—the Psalms. I would suggest that the context for nurturing the exploration of Old Testament theology is precisely the context in which the Psalms influenced the ancient community, the liturgical context. The singing and confessing of the ancient community's songs of faith expressed their faith but also helped them to embrace their faith and remember its stories and poems. These powerful songs kept them on the path of faith and kept them going in faith. The liturgical psalms nurtured their memories, their narrative constructs, their poetic images, and the community in the faith. That setting of the Psalms seems the most fruitful setting still for exploring Old Testament theology and its life-shaping cultural memory.

Some readers will be interested in the question of how Old Testament theology relates to the New Testament. Some Christian Old Testament theologians have addressed that question. Most of them today see considerable continuity between the testaments. The New Testament often quotes the Old. Claus Westermann notes that covenant and creation emphases continue in the New Testament.[1] One could think of Jesus as the one who comes to deliver in the narrative of the Synoptic Gospels. The Gospel of John includes wisdom and creation emphases. The epistolary material of the New Testament is

1. Westermann, *Old Testament and Jesus Christ*.

occasional literature dealing with early church issues and is in that sense analogous to the prophetic books. It is fair to say that interpreters cannot rightly understand the New Testament without understanding the Old Testament; the Old Testament is essential to study of the New Testament. A complex approach is best in thinking about how the testaments relate. The New Testament clearly emphasizes continuity with the Hebrew Scriptures; it also emphasizes continuity between the church and the faith community named Israel. The story of the divine-human encounter continues. A relationship of mutuality might be the best model. Theological claims in the Older Testament are taken up and continued in the New. The story of Jesus Christ and of the early Christian community hearkens back to the God-Israel relationship in the Hebrew Bible. The testaments stand in creative tension and in continuity with each other.

The plea of this author to you as readers is that you will pursue the theology of the Older Testament in terms of individual texts and their theological claims and in terms of theological frameworks and methods. Both are important. This volume's textual starting point provides an appropriate place for wisdom and addresses the diverse theological perspectives in the divine-human engagement. It can offer you much in exploring these fascinating narratives and poems of revelation and response. Good reading and good interpreting to you!

Bibliography

Albright, W. F. *From the Stone Age to Christianity: Monotheism and the Historical Process*. Garden City, NY: Doubleday, 1957.

Alter, Robert. *The Art of Biblical Narrative*. Rev. ed. New York: Basic Books, 2011.

———. *The Art of Biblical Poetry*. Rev. ed. New York: Basic Books, 2011.

Anderson, Bernhard W. *Contours of Old Testament Theology*. With the assistance of Steven Bishop. Minneapolis: Fortress, 1999.

Anderson, G. W. "Israel's Creed: Sung, Not Signed." *Scottish Journal of Theology* 16 (1963): 277–85.

Arterbury, Andrew E., W. H. Bellinger Jr., and Derek Dodson. *Engaging the Christian Scriptures: An Introduction to the Bible*. 2nd ed. Grand Rapids: Baker Academic, 2021.

Bailey, Randall, ed. *Yet with a Steady Beat: Contemporary U.S. Afrocentric Biblical Interpretation*. Semeia Studies. Atlanta: Society of Biblical Literature, 2003.

Barmash, Pamela. "The Narrative Quandary: Cases of Law in Literature." *Vetus Testamentum* 54 (2004): 1–16.

Barr, James. *The Concept of Biblical Theology: An Old Testament Perspective*. Minneapolis: Augsburg, 1999.

Bartor, Assnat. *Reading Law as Narrative: A Study in the Casuistic Laws of the Pentateuch*. Ancient Israel and Its Literature 5. Atlanta: Society of Biblical Literature, 2010.

Bauer, Georg Lorenz. *Theologie des Alten Testaments*. 2 vols. Leipzig: Weyand, 1796.

Bellinger, William H., Jr. "Portraits of Faith: The Scope of Theology in the Psalms." In *An Introduction to Wisdom Literature and the Psalms*, edited by Wayne Ballard and Dennis Tucker Jr., 111–28. Macon, GA: Mercer University Press, 2000.

———. *Psalms as a Grammar for Faith: Prayer and Praise*. Waco: Baylor University Press, 2019.

———. "The Psalms as a Place to Begin for Old Testament Theology." In *Psalms and Practice: Worship, Virtue, and Authority*, edited by Stephen Breck Reid, 28–39. Collegeville, MN: Liturgical Press, 2001.

———. "A Shape for Old Testament Theology: A Lost Cause?" *Perspectives in Religious Studies* 34 (2007): 287–95.

Bergmann, Michael, Michael J. Murray, and Michael C. Rea. *Divine Evil? The Moral Character of the God of Abraham*. Oxford: Oxford University Press, 2011.

Brettler, Marc Zvi. "A Jewish Approach to Psalm 111." In *Jewish and Christian Approaches to Psalms*, edited by Yair Zacovitch and Marianne Grohmann, 141–59. New York: Herder, 2009.

———. "Jewish Theology of the Psalms." In *The Oxford Handbook of the Psalms*, edited by William P. Brown, 485–98. Oxford: Oxford University Press, 2014.

Bright, John. *The Authority of the Old Testament*. Nashville: Abingdon, 1967.

Brooks, Peter. "Narrativity of the Law." *Law and Literature* 14 (2002): 1–10.

Brown, William P. *A Handbook to Old Testament Exegesis*. Louisville: John Knox, 2017.

———. *Seeing the Psalms: A Theology of Metaphor*. Louisville: John Knox, 2002.

Brueggemann, Walter. "A Convergence in Recent Old Testament Theologies." *Journal for the Study of the Old Testament* 18 (1980): 2–18.

———. "The Costly Loss of Lament." *Journal for the Study of the Old Testament* 11 (1986): 57–71.

———. "Kerygma of the Priestly Writer." *Zeitschrift für die alttestamentliche Wissenschaft* 84 (1972): 397–414.

———. "A Shape for Old Testament Theology, 1: Structure Legitimation." *Catholic Biblical Quarterly* 47 (1985): 28–46.

———. *Theology of the Old Testament: Testimony, Dispute, Advocacy*. Minneapolis: Fortress, 1997.

Brueggemann, Walter, and Tod Linafelt. *An Introduction to the Old Testament: The Canon and Christian Imagination*. 2nd ed. Louisville: Westminster John Knox, 2003.

Bultmann, Rudolf. "Weissagung und Erfüllung." *Zeitschrift für Theologie und Kirche* 47, no. 3 (1950): 360–83.

Childs, Brevard S. *Biblical Theology: A Proposal*. Facets. Minneapolis: Fortress, 2002.

———. *Biblical Theology in Crisis*. Philadelphia: Westminster, 1970.

———. *Exodus*. Old Testament Library. London: SCM, 1974.

———. *Introduction to the Old Testament as Scripture*. Philadelphia: Fortress, 1979.

———. *Old Testament Theology in a Canonical Context*. Philadelphia: Fortress, 1989.

———. "Wellhausen in English." *Semeia* 25 (1982): 83–88.

Clements, Ronald E. *A Century of Old Testament Study.* Cambridge: Lutterworth, 1976.

———. *Old Testament Theology: A Fresh Approach.* New Foundations Theological Library. Atlanta: John Knox, 1980.

———. *Prophecy and Covenant.* Louisville: Westminster John Knox, 1996.

Clines, David J. A. *The Theme of the Pentateuch.* 2nd ed. Sheffield: Sheffield Academic, 1997.

Collins, John J. *A Short Introduction to the Hebrew Bible.* 2nd ed. Minneapolis: Fortress, 2014.

Cover, Robert. "Nomos and Narrative." *Harvard Law Review* 97 (1983): 4–68.

Cross, Frank Moore. *Canaanite Myth and Hebrew Epic.* Cambridge, MA: Harvard University Press, 1973.

Dempsey, Carol J. *Earth, Wind, and Fire: Biblical and Theological Perspectives on Creation.* Edited by Carol J. Dempsey and Mary Margaret Pazdan. Collegeville, MN: Liturgical Press, 2004.

———. *Hope amid the Ruins: The Ethics of Israel's Prophets.* St. Louis: Chalice, 2000.

———. *The Prophets: A Liberation-Critical Reading.* Minneapolis: Fortress, 2000.

———. "The 'Whore' of Ezekiel 16: The Impact and Ramifications of Gender-Specific Metaphors in Light of Biblical Law and Divine Judgment." In *Gender and Law in the Hebrew Bible and the Ancient Near East,* 57–78. Sheffield: Sheffield Academic, 1998.

Eichrodt, Walther. *Theology of the Old Testament.* Translated by J. A. Baker. 2 vols. OTL. Philadelphia: Westminster, 1961–67.

Felder, Cain Hope, ed. *Stony the Road We Trod: African American Biblical Interpretation.* Minneapolis: Augsburg Fortress, 1991.

Fishbane, Michael. *Biblical Interpretation in Ancient Israel.* Oxford: Clarendon, 1985.

———. *The Exegetical Imagination: On Jewish Thought and Theology.* Cambridge, MA: Harvard University Press, 1998.

———. *Sacred Attunement: A Jewish Theology.* Chicago: University of Chicago Press, 2007.

Foster, Robert L. *We Have Heard, O Lord: An Introduction to the Theology of the Psalter.* Lanham, MD: Fortress Academic, 2019.

Fretheim, Terence E. *God and World in the Old Testament: A Relational Theology of Creation.* Nashville: Abingdon, 2005.

Gerstenberger, Erhard. *Theologies in the Old Testament.* Translated by John Bowden. Minneapolis: Fortress, 2002.

Goldingay, John. *Old Testament Theology.* 3 vols. Downers Grove, IL: InterVarsity, 2003–9.

Gottwald, Norman. *The Tribes of Yahweh: A Sociology of the Religion of Liberated Israel, 1250–1050 BCE*. Sheffield: Sheffield Academic, 1999.

Gustafson, James M. "Varieties of Moral Discourse: Prophetic, Narrative, Ethical, and Policy." In *Seeking Understanding: The Stob Lectures, 1986–1998*, 43–76. Grand Rapids: Eerdmans, 2001.

Hahn, Herbert F. "Wellhausen's Interpretation of Israel's Religious History." In *Essays on Jewish Life and Thought: Presented in Honor of Salo Wittmayer Baron*, edited by Joseph L. Blau, Philip Friedman, Arthur Hertzberg, and Isaac Mendelsohn, 299–308. New York: Columbia University Press, 1959.

Halberstam, Chaya. "The Art of Biblical Law." *Prooftexts* 27 (2007): 345–64.

Hanson, Paul. *Dynamic Transcendence: The Correlation of Confessional Heritage and Contemporary Experience in a Biblical Model of Divine Activity*. Philadelphia: Fortress, 1978.

Hasel, Gerhard F. *Old Testament Theology: Basic Issues in the Current Debate*. 4th ed. Grand Rapids: Eerdmans, 1991.

Hayes, John H. "Wellhausen as a Historian of Israel." In *Julius Wellhausen and His "Prolegomena to the History of Israel,"* edited by Douglas A. Knight, 37–60. Semeia 25. Chico, CA: Scholars Press, 1983.

Heschel, Abraham Joshua. *The Prophets*. New York: Harper & Row, 1962.

Jacob, Edmond. *Theology of the Old Testament*. Translated by Arthur W. Heathcote and Philip A. Allcock. London: Hodder & Stoughton, 1958. Originally published as *Théologie de l'ancien Testament* (Neuchâtel: Delachaux et Niestle, 1955).

Kelly, George A. *A Theory of Personality: The Psychology of Personal Constructs*. Norton Library. New York: Norton & Company, 1963.

Kessler, John. *Old Testament Theology: Divine Call and Human Response*. Waco: Baylor University Press, 2013.

Knierim, Rolf P. *The Task of Old Testament Theology: Substance, Method and Cases*. Grand Rapids: Eerdmans, 1995.

Köhler, Ludwig. *Old Testament Theology*. Translated by A. S. Todd. Philadelphia: Westminster Press, 1957. Reprint, Cambridge: James Clarke, 2003. Originally published as *Theologie des Alten Testament* (Tübingen: P. Siebeck, 1936).

Levenson, Jon D. *Creation and the Persistence of Evil: The Jewish Drama of Divine Omnipotence*. Princeton: Princeton University Press, 1994.

———. *Resurrection and the Restoration of Israel: The Ultimate Victory of the God of Life*. New Haven: Yale University Press, 2006.

———. "Why Jews Are Not Interested in Biblical Theology." In *Judaic Perspectives on Ancient Israel*, edited by Jacob Neusner, Baruch A. Levine, Ernest S. Frerichs, and Caroline McCracken-Flesher, 281–307. Philadelphia: Fortress, 1987.

Luther, Martin. "The Distinction between the Law and the Gospel: A Sermon Preached on January 1, 1532." Translated by Willard L. Bruce. *Concordia Journal* 18 (1992): 153–63.

———. *Dr. Martin Luthers Sämmtliche Schriften*. Edited by Johann Georg Walch. St. Louis: Concordia, 1910.

McEntire, Mark. *Portraits of a Mature God: Choices in Old Testament Theology*. Minneapolis: Fortress, 2013.

McLaughlin, John L. *An Introduction to Israel's Wisdom Traditions*. Grand Rapids: Eerdmans, 2018.

Milgrom, Jacob. "Law and Narrative and the Exegesis of Leviticus XIX 19." *Vetus Testamentum* 46 (1996): 544–48.

Miller, Patrick D. *The Lord of the Psalms*. Louisville: Westminster John Knox, 2013.

Moberly, R. W. L. *Old Testament Theology: Reading the Hebrew Bible as Christian Scripture*. Grand Rapids: Baker Academic, 2013.

Mowinckel, Sigmund. *The Psalms in Israel's Worship*. Vol. 1. Translated by D. R. Ap-Thomas. Oxford: Blackwell, 1962.

Nasuti, Harry. "Identity, Identification, and Imitation: The Narrative Hermeneutics of Biblical Law." *Journal of Law and Religion* 4 (1986): 9–23.

Neimeyer, Robert A., and Greg J. Neimeyer, eds. *Personal Construct Therapy Casebook*. New York: Springer Publishing, 1987.

Noth, Martin. *The Deuteronomistic History*. 2nd ed. Journal for the Study of the Old Testament Supplement Series 15. Sheffield: Sheffield Academic, 1981. Originally published as *Überlieferungsgeschichtliche Studien*, 2nd ed., 1–110 (Tübingen: Max Niemeyer Verlag, 1957).

Perdue, Leo G. *The Collapse of History: Reconstructing Old Testament Theology*. Overtures to Biblical Theology. Minneapolis: Fortress Augsburg, 1994.

———. *Reconstructing Old Testament Theology: After the Collapse of History*. Overtures to Biblical Theology. Minneapolis: Fortress Augsburg, 2005.

Rendtorff, Rolf. *Canon and Theology: Overtures to an Old Testament Theology*. Translated and edited by Margaret Kohl. Minneapolis: Fortress, 1993.

———. *The Canonical Hebrew Bible: A Theology of the Old Testament*. Translated by David Orton. Leiden: Deo, 2005.

Rogerson, John. *A Theology of the Old Testament: Cultural Memory, Communication, and Being Human*. Minneapolis: Fortress, 2010.

Römer, Thomas. *Dark God: Cruelty, Sex, and Violence in the Old Testament*. 3rd ed. Translated by Sean O'Neill. New York: Paulist Press, 2013.

Sanders, James A. "Adaptable for Life: The Nature and Function of Canon." In *Magnalia Dei: The Mighty Acts of God; Essays on the Bible and Archaeology in Memory of G. Ernest Wright*, edited by Frank Moore Cross et al., 531–60. Garden City, NY: Doubleday, 1976.

———. *Torah and Canon*. Philadelphia: Fortress, 1972.

Sandys-Wunsch, John, and Laurence M. Eldridge. "J. P. Gabler and the Distinction between Biblical and Dogmatic Theology." *Scottish Journal of Theology* 33 (1980): 133–58.

Schmid, Hans Heinrich. "Creation, Righteousness, and Salvation: 'Creation Theology' and the Broad Horizon of Biblical Theology." In *Creation in the Old Testament*, edited by Bernhard W. Anderson, 102–17. Philadelphia: Fortress, 1984.

Schmid, Konrad. *A Historical Theology of the Hebrew Bible*. Translated by Peter Altmann. Grand Rapids: Eerdmans, 2019. Originally published as *Theologie des Alten Testaments* (Tübingen: Mohr Siebeck, 2018).

———. *Is There Theology in the Hebrew Bible?* Winona Lake, IN: Eisenbrauns, 2015.

Seibert, Eric A. *Disturbing Divine Behavior: Troubling Old Testament Images of God*. Minneapolis: Fortress, 2009.

———. *The Violence of Scripture: Overcoming the Old Testament's Troubling Legacy*. Minneapolis: Fortress, 2012.

Seitz, Christopher. *Elder Testament: Canon, Theology, Trinity*. Waco: Baylor University Press, 2018.

Semler, J. S. *Abhandlung von freier Untersuchung des Kanon*. Halle, 1771–75.

Smith, Mark. *The Priestly Vision of Genesis 1*. Minneapolis: Fortress, 2010.

Strawn, Brent A. *The Old Testament Is Dying: A Diagnosis and Recommended Treatment*. Grand Rapids: Baker Academic, 2017.

Sweeney, Marvin A. *Reading the Hebrew Bible after the Shoah: Engaging Holocaust Theology*. Minneapolis: Fortress, 2008.

———. *Tanak: A Theological and Critical Introduction to the Jewish Bible*. Minneapolis: Fortress, 2012.

———. "Why Jews Are Interested in Biblical Theology: A Retrospective on the Work of Jon D. Levenson." *Jewish Book Annual* 55–56 (1997–99): 135–68.

Terrien, Samuel L. *The Elusive Presence: Toward a New Biblical Theology*. 3rd ed. Religious Perspectives. Eugene, OR: Wipf & Stock, 2000.

Trible, Phyllis. *God and the Rhetoric of Sexuality*. Overtures to Biblical Theology. Philadelphia: Fortress, 1978.

———. *Texts of Terror: Literary-Feminist Readings of Biblical Narratives*. Philadelphia: Fortress, 1984.

Udvari-Solner, Alice. *Joyful Learning: Active and Collaborative Learning in Inclusive Classrooms*. Thousand Oaks, CA: Corwin Press, 2008.

Vischer, Wilhelm Eduard. *Das Christuszeugnis des Alten Testaments*. 2 vols. Zürich: Zollikon, 1934, 1942.

von Rad, Gerhard. "The Form-Critical Problem of the Hexateuch." In *The Problem of the Hexateuch, and Other Essays*, 1–78. New York: McGraw-Hill, 1966.

————. "The Joseph Narrative and Ancient Wisdom." In *Studies in Ancient Israelite Wisdom*, edited by James L. Crenshaw, 439–47. New York: Ktav, 1976. English translation of "Josephgeschichte und altere Chokma." In *Congress Volume: Copenhagen 1953*, edited by G. W. Anderson, Aage Bentzen, P. A. H. de Boer, Millar Burrows, Henri Cazelles, and Martin Noth, 121–27. Supplements to Vetus Testamentum 1. Leiden: Brill, 1953.

————. *Old Testament Theology*. 2 vols. New York: Harper & Row, 1962–65. Originally published as *Theologie des Alten Testaments* (Munich: Kaiser Verlag, 1957–60).

————. "Typological Interpretation of the Old Testament." *Interpretation* 15 no. 2 (1961): 174–92.

————. *The Witness of the Old Testament to Christ*. Vol. 1, *The Pentateuch*. Translated by A. B. Crabtree. London: Lutterworth, 1949.

Vriezen, Theodorus C. *An Outline of Old Testament Theology*. 2nd ed. Oxford: Blackwell, 1970. First published 1958.

Ward, Ian. *Law and Literature: Possibilities and Perspectives*. New York: Cambridge University Press, 1995.

Wardlaw, Terence R., Jr. *Elohim within the Psalms: Petitioning the Creator to Order Chaos in Oral-Delivered Literature*. The Library of Hebrew Bible/Old Testament Studies. London: Bloomsbury T&T Clark, 2015.

Weems, Renita. *Battered Love: Marriage, Sex, and Violence in the Hebrew Prophets*. Minneapolis: Fortress, 1995.

Wellhausen, Julius. *Prolegomena to the History of Israel*. 3rd ed. Translated by John Sutherland Black and Allan Menzies. Edinburgh: Adam and Charles Black, 1885.

West, Robin. *Narrative, Authority, and Law*. Law, Meaning, and Violence. Ann Arbor: University of Michigan Press, 1993.

Westermann, Claus. *Blessing in the Bible and the Life of the Church*. Overtures to Biblical Theology. Philadelphia: Fortress, 1978.

————. *Elements of Old Testament Theology*. Atlanta: John Knox, 1982.

————. *The Old Testament and Jesus Christ*. Minneapolis: Augsburg, 1970.

————. *Praise and Lament in the Psalms*. Translated by Keith R. Crim and Richard N. Soulen. Atlanta: John Knox, 1981.

————. *What Does the Old Testament Say about God?* Atlanta: John Knox, 1979.

Wolff, Hans Walter. *Amos the Prophet*. Minneapolis: Fortress, 1973.

————. "The Kerygma of the Yahwist." *Interpretation* 20 (1966): 131–58.

Wright, George Ernest. *God Who Acts: Biblical Theology as a Recital*. Chicago: H. Regnery, 1952.

Zimmerli, Walther. *Old Testament Theology in Outline*. Translated by David E. Green. Atlanta: John Knox, 1978. Reprint, Edinburgh: T&T Clark, 2000. Originally published as *Grundriss der Alttestamentlichen Theologie* (Stuttgart: Kohlhammer, 1972).

Subject Index

Abrahamic covenant, 95
Abram, call of, 50, 76
Abram and Sarai, 75–77, 78
Achan, 102
'adam/'adamah, 71
African American interpreters, 30
Ai, 102
Albright, W. F., 26
Alter, Robert, 30n33
Amos, 59, 162–64
ancient Near East, 69
Anderson, Bernhard, 45, 47, 120
Anderson, George W., 45–47
anti-Semitism, 41n49
apocalyptic literature, 147, 148
ark of the covenant, 90, 101, 107
Assyrians, 116, 166, 169

Baal, 108, 112, 160
Babylonians, 116, 155, 166, 169
Balaam, 91–92
barrenness, 77–78
Bauer, G. L., 22
biblical theology movement, 21, 25–26

blessing, 9, 70
of all families of the earth, 76
through fertility of the land, 93and
fullness of life, 132, 166, 168
in Genesis, 80
neither controllable nor explainable in
human terms, 143
as sign of wisdom, 79
Brettler, Marc, 30
Bright, John, 26
Brown, William, 47
Brueggemann, Walter, 20, 24, 30, 31–32,
38, 40, 41, 42, 53, 175
burnt offering, 87

Cain and Abel, 74, 75
Calvin, John, 20
camp, order of, 90–91
Canaan. *See* land of Canaan
canon, 35–36
Christian, 27
context of exegesis and theological
reflection, 175
formation, 26–27
Hebrew, 99

censuses, in Numbers, 90–92
center of Old Testament faith (*die Mitte*), 23–24, 41, 47
cereal offering, 87
Childs, Brevard, 21, 26, 32, 35, 36, 40, 41, 42, 53, 175
Chronicles, covenant and creation theologies in, 114
church, nurtured and guided by Older Testament, xii–xiii
Clements, Ronald, 27
cold histories, 37
communities of faith, and theology of the Hebrew Scriptures, xii
community
  in covenant relationship, 102
  downward spiral of covenant faithlessness, 105
compensation offering, 87
completing creation, 35
continuing creation, 35
courtroom metaphor, 31, 41, 175
covenant
  blessing and cursing, 103
  as center of Old Testament theology, 41
  as contractual theology, 7
  faithfulness, 103, 111, 113, 158, 162, 169
  instruction. See *torah* (covenant instruction)
  relationship, as dialogical, 85
  renewal, 114, 159, 167
  See also covenant theology
Covenant Code, 55, 56, 83–84, 97
covenant theology, 2, 4
  and deliverance, 49, 53, 55, 172–73
  in Deuteronomy, 5
  in Exodus, 5
  in the Psalms, 4, 176
creation/blessing, 28–29
creation theology, 2, 4, 35
  and blessing, 51, 53, 55, 172
  in Genesis, 5

in the Psalter, 4, 125–29, 176
  and ritual purity, 88–89
Cross, F. M., 100n1
cult, 85, 168
cultural memory, 37
Cyrus, 156

Dagon, 107
Dame Folly, 138
Daniel, 147–48, 150
David
  as king, 110
  sin with Bathsheba, 14
Davidic covenant, 6, 106, 110, 153, 169
Davidic kingdom, 100, 101n1, 116
Day of Atonement, 88–89
day of YHWH, 161, 162, 164
days of creation, literary structure of, 68
Deborah, 103
Decalogue, 55, 56, 83–84
deliverance, 125. *See also* God: who delivers
deliverance of the Hebrews. *See* exodus from Egypt
Deuteronomistic History, 37, 100n1
Deuteronomy
  creation theology in, 92–94
  covenant theology in, 5, 92–94, 95
  influence on Former Prophets, 99
  prophetic theology in, 95
divine address. *See* God: who speaks
divine-human engagement, xi, 3, 40, 48–52, 62, 173–79
  in the Psalms, 118, 124, 131
divine presence
  centrality in the tabernacle, 90
  human need for, 15, 122
  "tabernacling" of, 85, 95
  and wholeness of life, 9, 85–86, 128–29
divine revelation and human response. *See* revelation and response

divine vengeance, 124
dominion, 67
dynamic analogy, 11–12

Ecclesiastes, 6, 143–45
Edomites, 164
Eichrodt, Walther, 20, 22–23, 24–26, 28, 32, 38, 40, 41, 42, 47, 53, 175
Elijah, 112
Eliphaz, Bildad, and Zophar, 142
Elisha, 112–13
endurance of Job, 143
Enlightenment, 21
entrance liturgies (Psalms), 51, 60
Enuma Elish, 69
Esau, 77, 164
eschatology, 35
Esther, 113, 114–15, 177
exile, 52, 99, 113, 116, 156, 164, 169–70
Exodus (book), 56
    covenant theology in, 5, 80–86, 95, 174
    lament in, 81, 95
exodus from Egypt, 5, 48, 55, 80–83, 94, 156, 172
Ezekiel, 6, 158–59
    creation and covenant theologies in, 159
    example of contextual theology, 159
    priestly perspective of, 6, 153, 159, 169–70
Ezra, 114

faith community, call to fidelity, 5
family, 168
"fear of the LORD," 138
feasts, 89–90
fertility religion, 93, 160, 169
firstborn, death of, 82
Fishbane, Michael, 30
form criticism, xi

Former Prophets, x, 5–6, 57, 99, 153, 168, 175
    covenant theology in, 100–101
    on the monarchy, 108, 109
Foster, Robert L., 118–19
founding memories, 37
Fretheim, Terence, 29, 34–35
fruitfulness, 70

Gabler, Johann Philipp, 21, 175
garden of Eden, 71, 73
genealogies, in primeval history, 66
"generations of the heavens and the earth," 71
Genesis, creation theology in, 5, 56, 66–80, 94–95, 174
Gerstenberger, Erhard, 27–28, 33–34
Gideon, 103
God
    diversity of portrayals in Old Testament, 38
    faithfulness of, 101n1
    source of wisdom, 136
    who blesses, 4, 49–51, 93, 94–95
    who delivers, 4, 8, 26, 48–49, 95
    who speaks, 5, 51, 58–60, 153, 170, 175
God and creatures, interrelatedness of, 35
"God at the end of history," 38
golden calf, 56, 91
Goldingay, John, 30n33, 34
Gottwald, Norman, 27
grace, power of, 75
Gunkel, Hermann, 61
Gustafson, James, 174

Habakkuk, 166
Haggai, 167
Hanson, Paul, 28, 54
"Harvard School," 100n1
Hebrew Bible, x
Hebrew narrative, 30

hermeneutic, for reading Scripture, 97–98
hermeneutics, 10–16
Heschel, Abraham Joshua, 57, 58, 163
Historical Books, 99–100, 116
historical-critical scholarship, 39, 41
history/deliverance, 28–29
history of traditions approach, 25–26
Hittite treaty formulas, 103
holiness, as human response to divine
    revelation, 89–90
Holiness Code, 89
hope, 168, 154, 164, 170
Hosea, 160
hot histories, 37

I AM WHO I AM, 81
idolatry, 4, 52, 59, 93, 112, 154, 158–59,
    162, 166, 169, 170
image of God, 67–69
imagery, 14–15
imagination, 14
implicit and explicit theology, 39
imprecatory psalms, 124–25
impurity, 88–89
injustice, 4, 154, 168, 169
instruction. See torah (covenant
    instruction)
integrity, 2
interpreters, backgrounds and convic-
    tions of, 34, 40–41
Isaac, 77
Isaiah, 6, 154–57, 169
    creation and covenant theologies in, 156
    as exilic voice of the prophet, 59
    on Israel as a vineyard, 15
    prophetic theology in, 157
Ishmael, 77
Israel
    inability to exercise covenant faithful-
        ness, 107–8
    keeping covenant with YHWH, 105
    rebellion in the wilderness, 91–92

Jabesh-gilead, 104
Jacob, 76, 77, 78–79
Jacob, Edmond, 24
Jephthah, 103
Jeremiah, 6, 157–58, 169
Jericho, 102
Jeroboam, 101n1, 112
Jerusalem, fall of, 100, 101n1, 116, 146
Jesus, as deliverer, 178
Jewish community, exclusive or particu-
    larist approach of, 165
Jewish interpreters, 30, 41
Jezebel, 112
Job, 6, 141–43, 144
    suffering of, 141–42, 150
Jochebed, 82
Joel, 161
Jonah, 12, 164–65
Joseph, 76–77, 79, 80
Josiah, 101n1, 113
Judges, 103–5, 107
judgment, 7, 154, 163, 164, 170
justice, 162, 165, 166

Kessler, John, 11n2, 38
Ketuvim (Writings), x, 36
king
    Israel's request for, 107–8
    as YHWH's representative in ruling
        over people, 108
kingdom of God, coming of, 148, 150
Kings (books of), 6, 106–13
kings of Israel, covenant disobedience
    of, 111–12
Kliever, Lonnie, 30–31
Knierim, Rolf, 29
Köhler, Ludwig, 24, 40

Lamentations, 146
lament psalms, 4, 6, 48, 61, 119, 120,
    129, 133, 134, 142
    and covenant theology, 121–24

land of Canaan, 100
  distribution of, 102
  fertility of, 93
Latter Prophets, x, 4, 6, 9, 52, 57, 99,
    153, 168–69, 175, 177
law, in the Older Testament, 84
law codes. *See* Covenant Code
Leah, 78
legal matters, in Hebrew Bible, 13–14
Levenson, Jon, 30, 41n49
Lévi-Strauss, Claude, 37
Levite and his wife (Judges), 103–5
Levites, 90–91
Leviticus, covenant and creation theolo-
    gies in, 86
liberation theology, 31, 33, 134
life
  as a gift, 145
  ordering of, 142, 145
  wonders of, 146
life of faith, in already-but-not-yet,
    148
liturgical context, 15–16
locust plague, 161
Luther, Martin, 20, 47

McEntire, Mark, 38
Malachi, 168
manna, provision of, 91
Manual of Purity, 88–89
marriage, 168
matriarchs, 78
"mature God," 38
Megilloth, 146
memory, 15
messenger formula, 58
metaphorical theologies, 30
Micah, 165
"mighty acts of God," 38
Miriam, 82
Moberly, Walter, 38–39
modernism, 3

modernity, 21
Momaday, Scott, 16
monarchy, 100, 106
  and covenant theology, 111
  divided, 111–13
  as necessary evil, 105
  polemic in favor of, 105
  united, 109–11
Mosaic covenant. *See* Sinaitic covenant
Moses
  call of, 56
  leadership of, 82
Mowinckel, Sigmund, 96
mutuality of vocation, 35

Nahum, 166
Naomi, 115
narrative
  and memory, 15
  primary genre in the Older Testament,
    12–13
  in primeval history, 66–67
  shapes communities, 174
narrative coherence, 40
narrative theology, 30, 34, 37
Nathan, 110
Nazirites, 91
Nehemiah, 114
nephesh, 72
Nevi'im, x
new covenant, 158
new heaven and earth, 35
new song, 118, 119, 128, 157
New Testament, continuity with the
    Old, 178–79
Nineveh, 164–65
Noah and the flood, 74, 75
Noahic covenant, 95
Northern Kingdom (Israel), 100, 101n1,
    111–12
Noth, Martin, 100n1
Numbers, 90–92

Obadiah, 164
Old Testament
    diversity in, 31, 24–25, 33, 177
    as a term, ix–x
Old Testament theology
    bipolar theologies, 28–29, 54
    diachronic and synchronic ap-
        proaches, 24
    as lost cause, 32
    modern study, 3
    particularism and universalism in, 23,
        28
    pluralism in, 30–31
    recent works, 33–39
    tripartite shape, 55–58
oppression, 169
originating creation, 35
Othniel, 103

Passover, 82–83, 89–90
"patience of Job," 143
Pentateuch
    composition of, xi
    as identity-forming narrative, 96
Pentecost, 89
Perdue, Leo, 29–30, 40, 41, 176
Philistines, 107–8
plagues on Egypt, 81–82
poetry
    encountering mystery of revelatory
        texts, 98
    narrative impulse in, 13
postcolonial interpretation, 63n15
postmodern interpreters, 41, 63n15
Potiphar's wife, 77
practical wisdom, 6, 135, 139, 140, 141,
    146, 149–50
praise, as universal, 127–28
praise psalms, 4, 62, 118, 119, 125–29,
    130
Priestly theology, 153
    in Deuteronomy, 95
    in Ezekiel, 6, 153, 159, 169–70
    in Genesis 1, 70–71

primeval history, 66–75
prooftexting, 20
prophecy, 153–70
    as foretelling and forth-telling, 9
prophetic theology, 2, 4–5, 61, 153, 170
    addressed to Northern Kingdom,
        112–13
    addressed to Southern Kingdom, 113
    and God who speaks, 52, 53, 57–60,
        173
    in the Psalter, 176
prosperity, 169
Proverbs, 6, 144
    creation theology in, 137–40
    as pragmatic wisdom, 149–50
    wisdom of, 9
providence, 113, 115
psalm of Miriam/Moses, 82
Psalms
    as community's confession of faith,
        45–47, 117, 174, 176
    covenant theology in, 118, 119, 120–
        25, 133, 175
    creation theology in, 118, 119, 132–33,
        175
    as grammar of faith, 121
    portrayal of God in five books, 119
    prayer and praise in, 6, 10, 61, 120–22
    prophetic theology in, 60–61, 118,
        119, 129–31, 133–34
    singing of, 118, 128, 176, 178
Psalms of Ascent, 118
purification offering, 87

Qoheleth, 145, 150
quail, provision of, 91

Rabbinic Judaism, xii, 41n49
Rachel, 78
Rahab, 102
Rebecca, 77, 78
Rendtorff, Rolf, 27, 35–37

repentance, 4, 9–10, 107, 161, 167
   for Nineveh, 164–65
   response to prophetic theology, 52, 53,
      58, 60, 63, 153, 170, 173, 175
retributive justice, 162
revelation and response, 2, 10–11, 107,
   170, 172–73
ritual purity, and creation theology, 88–89
Rogerson, John, 37–38
royal psalms, 50, 119, 131–32
Ruth, 113, 115, 177

Sabbath, 70, 90
sacral kingship, 108
sacrifices, as human response to divine
   revelation, 86–87
salvation, as wholeness or fullness of
   life, 2, 8–10, 62, 63, 178
Samson, 103
Samuel (books of), 106–10
Sanders, James, 27
Sarai, 78
Saul, as covenant-breaking king, 109–10
Schmid, H. H., 29, 54
Schmid, Konrad, 39, 40
Sea of Reeds, 82
second exodus (from exile), 52, 59, 156
Second Temple Judaism, 57, 114–15
Semler, J. J., 21
shared offering, 87
"shattered spectrum," 31, 32, 41, 42, 176
Shechem, 79
Sheol, 125
Shiphrah and Puah, 82
sibling rivalry, 78–79
sin, 71–72, 75
Sinaitic covenant, 6, 66, 83–84, 106,
   110, 153, 169
social injustice, 52, 59, 162, 170
sociological reading, of Hebrew Scrip-
   tures, 27–28
Solomon, 110, 143

Song of Songs, 146–47
Songs of Ascent, 49–50
Southern Kingdom (Judah), 100, 101n1,
   111
speculative wisdom, 141, 150
stories, impact of, 16
Strawn, Brent, 19
suffering, 141–42
supersessionism, ix, xii
Sweeney, Marvin, 30
syncretism, 108, 160

tabernacle, 57, 85, 90
Tanak, x
temple
   as place of divine presence, 128
   rebuilding of, 114, 167
Ten Words. See Decalogue
Terrien, Samuel, 28, 40, 54
text
   and context, 33
   and readers, 32, 63n15, 98, 173
thanksgiving psalms, 126–27
theodicy, 6, 116, 141
theological education, xi
theological interpretation, 11, 36
theology, ix, xi
theophany at Sinai, 83
Torah, x, 5
torah (covenant instruction), 4, 5, 7–8,
   65, 84, 92–93
   faithfulness to, 110
   as a gift, 86, 132
   in the Psalms, 121
   as response to covenant theology, 49,
      53, 55, 62, 173
   written in the hearts of people, 158
Torah-Nevi'im-Ketuvim (the Law, the
   Prophets, and the Writings), x, 36
tower of Babel, 74–75
tree of the knowledge of good and evil,
   71
Twelve, 6, 159, 170

valley of dry bones, 158
vanity, 143, 145
von Rad, Gerhard, 20, 24–26, 29, 32, 38,
    40, 41, 42, 53, 54, 175
Vriezen, Theodorus, 24, 40

water, provision of, 91
Wellhausen, Julius, 22
Westermann, Claus, 28, 40, 49, 54, 178
wholeness of life, 2, 65, 95
    and covenant faithfulness, 103
    and divine presence, 85–86
wisdom, 4, 6, 43
    comes from experience or observa-
        tion, 136
    instructs in the life of faith, 136
    response to creation theology, 9, 51,
        53, 56, 62, 136–37, 149, 151, 172, 175
    rigid understanding of, 141
    tied to morality and justice, 136
Wisdom of Amenemope, 137
wisdom psalms, 50, 119, 132
wise and foolish, 138–40
Wolff, Hans Walter, 59

womanist theological perspectives, 30
Woman Wisdom, 15, 138–39, 140
women
    in exodus from Egypt, 82
    in Hebrew Scriptures, 30
worship, 129–30
    central to the Pentateuch, 96–97
    and ethical living, 83, 96
    as response to divine revelation, 85–86
worshiping community, 16, 45, 46, 47,
    52, 97
Wright, George Ernest, 26
Writings, 114, 135

Year of Jubilee, 90
YHWH, 81
    as jealous God, 94
YHWH-Israel "marriage," 160–61

Zechariah, 167–68
Zephaniah, 166–67
Zimmerli, Walther, 11n2, 24
Zion, 154–55

Scripture Index

Old Testament

Genesis

1 20, 37, 66, 71, 74
1–3 73
1–11 66, 67, 76
1:1–2 70
1:2 70
1:3–5 68
1:4 68
1:5 68
1:6–7 68
1:6–8 68
1:7 68
1:8 68
1:9–10 68
1:9–12 68
1:9–13 68
1:11–12 68
1:12 68
1:13 68
1:14–15 68
1:14–18 68
1:14–19 68
1:16–18 68
1:17–18 68
1:19 68

1:20–22 68
1:20–23 68
1:21 68
1:22 68, 70
1:23 68
1:24–25 68
1:24–30 68
1:24–31 68
1:25 68
1:26 69
1:26–28 68
1:27 67, 68, 73
1:28 50, 67, 68, 69, 70
1:29–30 68
1:31 68
2–3 66, 71–73, 75
2–11 75
2:1–3 70
2:1–4 70
2:3 70
2:4 71
2:7 72
2:17 73
3 71, 73
3:21 73
4 75
4–11 74–76

4:12 74
5 66
6–9 74, 75
8–9 37
9 74
10 66
11 66, 74, 75, 76
12 78, 80
12–50 66
12:1–3 50, 76, 79
12:2 77
12:10–20 77
15 77
15:5–7 76
16 77
17 56
17:2 76
17:5 77
17:7 76
17:19 76
17:21 76
20 78
22:15–19 77
25:21–22 78
26 78
26:24 76
27 77, 78

28:3–4 76
28:13–15 76
30:22–24 78
34 77, 79
48:16 76
50:20 79

Exodus

3 81, 82
3:7–9 48
3:14–15 81
9:14 81
14:21–31 82
14:31 82
15 35
19:6 86
20 7, 84
20:2 8
20:3 7, 83
20:22–23:19 83
24 85
25–40 56, 85
29:43–46 85
32–34 56
34 165
40:34–38 57, 85

Leviticus

1 87
1:1–6:7 87
2 87
3 87
4:1–5:13 87
5:14–6:7 87
6:8–7:38 87
11–15 88
12 88
13–14 88
15 88
17–26 89, 89n8
18:1–5 89

18:24–30 89
23 89
24:1–9 90
25 90

Numbers

1–10 90
6 91
10 91
22–24 91
26 92

Deuteronomy

4:34 92
5:7 103
5:15 92
6 121
6:4 94
6:4–5 92
7:12–14 93
7:19 92
11:2–4 92
12:5 92
12:11 92
12:21 92
14:23–24 92
16:2 92
16:6 92
16:11 92
17:14–20 109, 111
26:2 92
26:5–10 25
26:8 92
27–28 93
27:9–10 94
30:15–20 93

Joshua

1–12 102
5 102

6 102
21:43–45 102
24:14–15 101
24:16 103

Judges

2 103
19–21 103, 105
19:22 104
21:25 105

1 Samuel

4–6 107
8–9 108
13 110
15 110

2 Samuel

7 110

1 Kings

3 110
18 112
21 112

2 Kings

22–23 113

Nehemiah

1:5 114

Job

1:1 141
1:9 141
3 20, 143
7 20
28 142, 143
38–41 37, 142, 143

Psalms

1–2 36
1–41 117
2 117, 118, 131, 132
8 20, 133
15 51, 60, 129
15:1–2 130
19 132
19:1 132
24 60, 129
24:1 133
24:3–4 51, 130
24:4 51
30:6–7 126
30:8–10 126–27
30:11 127
37 132
42 14, 122
42–72 117
45 131
46 128
46:4 128
48 128
48:9 129
49 132
50 60, 130
50:7 51, 61
50:7–15 130
50:15 130
50:16–23 130
73 132
73–89 117
74 117
78 132
79 117
81 60, 130
81:5 61, 130
81:11–13 51–52
82 60, 130
82:1 61
82:3–4 130–31

82:6 61
89 117, 131
90–106 118
93–100 118, 128
95 60, 130, 131
95:7 61
96:1 128
96:5–6 128
104:24 133
107–50 118
107:6 48
109 124
109:6 124
109:8–12 124
112 132
117 127
119 118, 132
120–34 118
127 132
128 132
133 132
134:3 49
137 125
148:5 133
150 36

Proverbs

1–9 139, 140
3:19–22 137
8:22 138
8:29–31 138
8:32–36 139
10:18 139
11:1 140
14:16 140
16:8 139
16:18 139
17:12 140
17:22 139
22:17–24:22 137
26:11 139
27:14 139

27:23–27 140
30–31 140

Ecclesiastes

1 37
1:14 143
2:11 143
2:17 143
2:26 143
4:4 143
4:16 143
6:9 143
6:12 145
7:15–18 145
8:17 145
10:14 145

Song of Songs

2:8–9 146–47
4:1 147

Isaiah

1:16–17 155
1:27 155
2 155
40 156
40–55 52, 59, 157
53:5–7 156
56–66 157

Jeremiah

7 158
7:5–7 170
18:11 170
31 158

Ezekiel

37 158
37:27 158

Daniel

1:20 148
2 148
6:25–28 148
7:14 148

Hosea

4:2 59
4:3 59, 161
6:1 59
11 161
14 161
14:1 59, 170
14:9 160

Joel

3:16 161

Amos

1–2 163
1:2 161, 163
2:4 163

2:10 163
3 163
3:1 164
3:2 162
3:3–8 164
4:1 164
4:13 59, 163
5:1 164
5:8–9 59, 163
5:24 162
9:5–6 59, 163
9:7–8 163

Jonah

4 165

Micah

6:1–8 165
6:8 165

Zephaniah

3:19 167

Zechariah

1:3–4 168
9:9 167

Malachi

1:5 168
1:14 168
2:10 168
3:5 168
3:7 170
3:14 168
3:18 168
4:4 168

New Testament

James

5:11 143

DATE DUE
